T0323910

THE BEHAVIOR GAP

THE BEHAVIOR GAP

CARL RICHARDS

SIMPLE WAYS TO STOP DOING DUMB THINGS WITH MONEY

Portfolio/Penguin

PORTFOLIO / PENGUIN
Published by the Penguin Group
Penguin Group (USA) Inc., 375 Hudson Street, New York, New York 10014, U.S.A. • Penguin Group (Canada), 90 Eglinton Avenue East, Suite 700, Toronto, Ontario, Canada M4P 2Y3 (a division of Pearson Penguin Canada Inc.) • Penguin Books Ltd, 80 Strand, London WC2R 0RL, England • Penguin Ireland, 25 St. Stephen's Green, Dublin 2, Ireland (a division of Penguin Books Ltd) • Penguin Books Australia Ltd, 250 Camberwell Road, Camberwell, Victoria 3124, Australia (a division of Pearson Australia Group Pty Ltd) • Penguin Books India Pvt Ltd, 11 Community Centre, Panchsheel Park, New Delhi—110 017, India • Penguin Group (NZ), 67 Apollo Drive, Rosedale, Auckland 0632, New Zealand (a division of Pearson New Zealand Ltd) • Penguin Books (South Africa) (Pty) Ltd, 24 Sturdee Avenue, Rosebank, Johannesburg 2196, South Africa

Penguin Books Ltd, Registered Offices:
80 Strand, London WC2R 0RL, England

First published in 2012 by Portfolio / Penguin,
a member of Penguin Group (USA) Inc.

Some of the drawings in this book first appeared in *The New York Times*.

Publisher's Note
This publication is designed to provide accurate and authoritative information in regard to the subject matter covered. It is sold with the understanding that the publisher is not engaged in rendering legal, accounting or other professional services. If you require legal advice or other expert assistance, you should seek the services of a competent professional.

LIBRARY OF CONGRESS CATALOGING-IN-PUBLICATION DATA

Richards, Carl, 1972–
The behavior gap : simple ways to stop doing dumb things with money / Carl Richards.
p. cm.
1. Finance, Personal. 2. Investments. 3. Portfolio management. I. Title.
HG179.R447 2012
332.024—dc23
2011033413

Paperback ISBN: 979-8-217-04678-2

Set in Bell MT Std
Designed by Spring Hoteling

148720106

For

Cori

&

Lindsay, Grace, Samuel, and Ruby Jane

CONTENTS

INTRODUCTION
FOUR PAIRS OF SKIS

THIS is a book about how you can make good money decisions.

I am not talking about which investment to buy or how much to invest in the stock market.

I am talking about *decisions that are in tune with reality, with your goals, and with your values.*

Why would anyone not make decisions that way?

Well, we get confused. We get scared. We get carried away.

That's why this is also a book about how to avoid confusion, how to cope with fear, and how to stay grounded when making financial choices.

That sounds hard—and as we'll see, it's not always easy. But it's pretty simple. In fact, simplicity is one of the keys.

I live in Park City, Utah, where some of us take skiing pretty seriously. One morning some years back, a friend swung by my house to pick me up to go backcountry skiing.

I ran into the garage to grab my skis. I stood there for a second looking at my four different pairs of skis, each designed for particular conditions, and suddenly, I was paralyzed. I just couldn't choose.

My friend sat in the car honking the horn—*Let's go, Carl! Move it! The sun's coming up! The snow's getting soft!*—while I stared at those skis. It was ridiculous. I'd spent all that money and time and energy collecting these skis so I would be ready to deal with any situation—and now I just felt powerless.

That day was a turning point for me. I got rid of three pairs of skis, and kept my favorite pair: the ones that would let me do what I really care about doing, which is to move light and fast through the backcountry.

The skis I kept aren't perfect in every condition. They're actually a pretty bad solution in heavy snow or in really steep terrain. So what? They're a decent compromise in most situations, and they work beautifully in the conditions I like best.

Now I don't have to think about which skis to bring on a trip. I just grab the ones I have and go. I trust my experience and my instincts and my luck to make it through situations when my equipment isn't perfect.

Lots of people think that to make good money decisions you need to have a plan for every situation. You need insurance for every possible setback, and investments for every market condition. All of your assumptions about the future need to be refined to perfection, so that you will never be surprised. You need to know and understand everything about the financial markets, and you need to budget your spending to the last dime.

That kind of thinking is based on fear. We fear (naturally enough) life's uncertainty, its ups and downs. And so we make plans that we hope will give us the power to control our future. If I do this, that will not happen; if I sell now, I will avoid the coming downturn; if I pick the right investments, I will be financially safe; if I worry enough, I will be ready when bad news comes.

Trouble is, the real world is complicated: we don't know what's going to happen.

That means that most of our plans are useless. When I had four pairs of skis, I was always choosing the wrong ones anyway!

The point is, no plan will cover every situation—and that's okay. You don't have to choose the perfect investment or save exactly the right amount or predict your rate of return or spend hours watching television shows about the stock market or surfing the Internet for stock picks. You don't need a plan for every contingency.

So if planning isn't the solution to our money problems, what is? More simply, what can we do to get what we really want?

We can stop chasing fantasies. We are not going to get what we want by beating the market or picking the perfect investment or designing the perfect bulletproof financial plan. In fact, when we try to do those things we get into big trouble.

We can protect ourselves—to a point. Risk is what's

left when you think you've thought of everything. Our assumptions about the future are almost always wrong. We can never think of everything—but we can take sensible steps to protect ourselves from life's inevitable surprises.

We can embrace uncertainty. Change isn't always a problem. Many—perhaps most—of life's surprises are good news. If we aren't locked down into a rigid plan, we can recognize and seize opportunities when they come up.

We can decide what we really want. When someone asks you what you really want out of life, you're probably not going to say you want an investment that delivers good returns. Like the rest of us, you want to be happy and fulfilled. Your financial decisions should align with what you know about yourself and the world. The more you know about yourself, the more successful your investments will be—that is, the more they will align with your true goals as a human being. Deciding what you really want takes an awful lot of work, which is one reason why most of us don't do it. But once you know what you (and your family) really want, you will know what to do—how much insurance to buy, where to invest your money, whether to quit your job and start a new venture.

We can make decisions that make sense. We can't control the markets or the economy, but our behavior is up to us. It's true that the outcomes of our decisions may vary. In fact, you can make a good decision and have a bad outcome. But sensible, reality-based choices are our best shot at reaching our goals.

We can trust our luck. Most financial planners don't

like to talk about luck. The idea that some things just happen by chance can be a scary one. But I think it's really cool that we don't control our destinies. We can stay open and respond creatively. And sometimes the things that happen to us are much better than anything we could plan ourselves.

My wife and I met at a ski shop when we were college students (luck). We married (smart behavior, at least on my part) in 1995, when I was still an undeclared major at the University of Utah and digging ditches for a landscaping company. Cori decided that digging ditches wasn't a long-term career path for me, and we found a want ad for what we thought was a job that had something to do with security—being a security guard? working with alarm systems?—you know, keeping things safe.

It turned out the job was in the securities *industry*, with a mutual fund company (luck). The interviewers narrowed the pool of applicants down to two of us. The other guy and I sat next to each other in a waiting room while they decided whom to hire.

The door opened. A young woman informed us that they'd picked the other guy. He looked at me and said, "I don't want it. You can have it" (luck).

So I got the job. I've spent the past fifteen years giving people financial advice. Every great thing that has happened (and there have been a bunch) has been at least partly a matter of luck. Even the setbacks have taught me important lessons, including some that I've tried to pass along in this book. One of those lessons is that you aren't in charge of everything. Do what you can, and then relax.

We can trust ourselves. Of course, luck is only part of it. One day my supervisor at that same mutual fund company informed me that my shift had changed, and I'd have to work on Sunday. I had other commitments on Sunday, and I told her so. She told me to choose, so I quit. That led to my next job, which led to my next, which led to my business, which eventually led to a regular blog for *The New York Times* and this book and all kinds of great stuff.

I stood by what really mattered to me—I wanted Sundays off—and I lost my job. What a disaster, right? And so far, at least, that decision—and that disaster—have made all the difference.

I don't believe that there is a secret to getting rich. But in the end, financial decisions aren't about getting rich. They're about getting what you want—getting happy. And if there is a secret to getting happy, it's this: be true to yourself.

Maybe you've heard that one before.

But I'll bet you haven't read it in a book about money.

WE DON'T BEAT THE MARKET,
THE MARKET BEATS US

THE BEHAVIOR GAP

COMPANIES like Morningstar and Dalbar have done a bunch of studies that try to quantify the impact of investor behavior on real-life returns. The studies typically compare investors' actual returns in stock funds to the average returns of the funds themselves. Just to be clear, they're trying to compare the returns *investors* get to the returns *investments* get.

Is there really a difference? Oh, you bet there is. Typically, the studies find that the returns investors have earned over time are much lower than the returns of the average investment.

What that means is that we're leaving money on the table.

Take mutual funds. All we had to do was simply put our money in an average stock mutual fund and let it sit there.

But most investors didn't do that. Instead, they moved their money in and out of stock funds. Their timing was miserable—and it cost them dearly.

I coined the term "behavior gap" to label the gap between investor returns and investment returns, and I started drawing the sketch you see here on every whiteboard I could find. Since then, I've used the behavior gap to describe all kinds of situations where our behavior leads us to subpar results, and I've drawn many sketches to help my clients and readers understand what's really driving their actions. But this sketch is the original.

It's clear that buying even an average mutual fund and holding on to it for a long time has been a pretty decent strategy. But real people don't invest that way. We trade. We

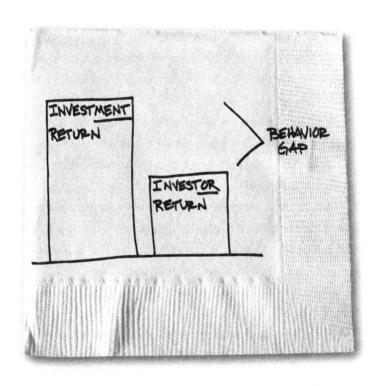

watch CNBC and listen to Jim Cramer yell. We buy what's up and sell what's down. In other words, we do exactly what we all know we shouldn't do.

I know it's time to be cautious when I get lots of emails from readers of my *New York Times* blog urging me to add stocks to my holdings. Likewise, I know it's probably a good time to be hopeful about the market's prospects when certain friends and colleagues are anxious to sell stocks.

What's incredible is that they know it, too! We laugh about it together. They know their impulses to buy and sell are dangerous. They rely on me to help them keep those impulses under control.

Back in the spring of 2009, my clients were very worried indeed. Three of them came in together to see me one day. Like most of us, they were scared to death. The market had plunged, and they'd sustained significant losses.

The conversation quickly turned to how scary the stock market was.

Them: *Hey, Carl, we think it's time to sell.*

Me: *Are you suggesting that we sell something simply because it's down 30 percent?*

Them: *Well . . . you know . . . are we just going to keep sitting here while this thing goes down?*

Me: *The damage has been done, guys. You may feel like selling, but does it make any sense to sell now?*

Them: *It's scary!*

Me: *It's okay to be scared, but it's a bad idea to act on your fear.*

Them: *But this is just too painful! If things continue at this rate we'll have no money by the end of the year!*

Me: *Actually, stocks were a lot riskier when they were more expensive. But back then, you were happy to hold them. Why sell now?*

Them*: So what do we do instead?*

My answer to that one was pretty simple. I told them we should do absolutely nothing. Instead, we'd wait for things to calm down a bit, and then review their plans to make sure they still made sense.

Fast-forward a couple of years. The same three guys came to see me again. Stocks had rebounded sharply, and we had a very different conversation.

Them: *Should we move more of our cash into stocks?*

Me: *Uh, why?*

Them: *Because the market's done so well lately!*

Me: *You mean you want to buy more stocks because stocks are more expensive?*

Them: *Well, they might keep going up!*

Me: *We have no idea what the market will do in the future. Why don't we stick with our plan?*

I have these conversations all the time. In early 2011, with gold up 80 percent over two-plus years, everyone wanted to know if they should be buying it. For a while that was the most common question I got.

I answered that gold was now riskier than it had been in a very long time. If it wasn't already part of their plan, why add it now?

My friends and clients (often the same people) aren't the

only investors tempted to do the wrong thing. In 2008, 2009, and most of 2010, mutual fund investors consistently took more money out of stock mutual funds than they added. In December 2010 alone, we pulled $10.6 billion out of equity mutual funds.

Then, in January 2011, someone hit a switch: that month, we poured an estimated $30 billion into the market. Investors had decided that it was time to get back into stocks. This decision came after an almost 100 percent gain from the market bottom in 2008.

Is it rational to pour money into an asset that has doubled in value in less than two years? Would you buy a house that had climbed in value from $300,000 to $600,000 in two years? (What's that? You did? How'd that work out?)

Let's go back to early 2000. The dot-com market is booming. The NASDAQ has gained better than 80 percent during the past year. People are borrowing against their home equity and using the cash to buy stocks—especially technology stocks.

Investors put close to $44 billion into stock mutual funds in January 2000, according to the Investment Company Institute, shattering the previous one-month record of $28.5 billion.

We all know the story from there. Money continued to pour into stock funds, breaking records for February and March. The NASDAQ climbed to 5,000, only to plummet, losing something like half its value by the end of the year.

But if you think we get irrational at market tops, wait until you see how we behave at market bottoms. October 2002 was the fifth month in a row that investors pulled more money out of stock mutual funds than they put into them—the first time ever such a streak had occurred.

Just take a wild guess at when the market hit bottom. October!

Stop and think about this for a second. At the market peak, we were borrowing against our homes to buy overpriced technology stocks. At the bottom, we couldn't sell stocks fast enough. And where was all the money going? Investors were using it to buy bond funds, which recorded record cash inflows during the period—even though bond prices were by some measures higher than they'd been in more than forty years.

This is nothing new. We do it all the time. We did it

with emerging markets in 2004, with real estate in 2006 and 2007 . . . Repeat until broke.

No wonder most people are unsatisfied with their investing experience.

The more expensive stocks (or houses) are, the more risky they are—yet that's when we tend to find them most attractive. In short, investors as a group tend to be horrendously bad at timing the market.

It makes far more sense to ignore what the crowd is doing and base your investment decisions on what you need to do to reach your goals. But man, is that hard to do.

It's not that we're dumb. We're wired to avoid pain and pursue pleasure and security. It feels right to sell when everyone around us is scared and buy when everyone feels great.

It may feel right. But it's not rational.

Invest*ment* Mistakes Are Invest*or* Mistakes

I am more convinced than ever that all invest*ment* mistakes are really invest*or* mistakes.

Investments don't make mistakes. Investors do.

When you invest, you're making a choice. That's the part we often forget. At some point, we said yes to the investment. We had control over everything leading up to that point. We decided which (if any) questions to ask about the investment. We decided whom to ask. We decided how much to invest and when to invest.

If an investment performs well, we like to think, "I picked a winner." And hey, it's nice to take credit when things go well.

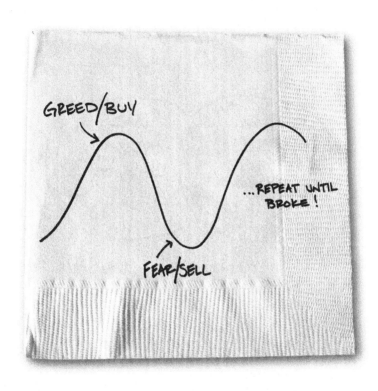

But when one of our investments tanks, it's someone else's fault. We blame the guy who sold it to us, the rogue investment bankers who wrecked the economy, out-of-control government spending, lies in the media, bad weather in Brazil . . . just about any scapegoat will do.

It all reminds me of that time I ran over a sprinkler head with my parents' lawn mower. I remember running inside to tell my mom that the lawn mower had hit the sprinkler. She patiently taught me that lawn mowers don't hit sprinklers; ten-year-old boys pushing lawn mowers do.

We do the same thing when it comes to investing. If we haven't done our research (figured out where the sprinklers are) and we behave poorly (run over the sprinklers), we're not going to like the results.

And we can't blame the investment for our decisions. At some point, we must accept responsibility. Otherwise we'll keep making the same mistake. And in that case, we might as well give up trying to invest, put all our savings in fixed-rate bank CDs, and go enjoy our lives.

One definition of insanity goes something like this: insanity is when you keep doing the same thing (in this case, blaming your investments for your losses) and expect a different result (in this case, good returns).

Let's stop acting crazy.

Long-Term Memory Loss

There are ways to try to close the behavior gap. But before we set out to change our behavior, we need to understand it.

For starters, there's that natural tendency of ours to

avoid pain and seek pleasure. Beyond that, we're downright terrible at predicting the future.

Boom-and-bust cycles are largely a function of our collective expectations. Expectations drive our behavior—but they are almost always wrong.

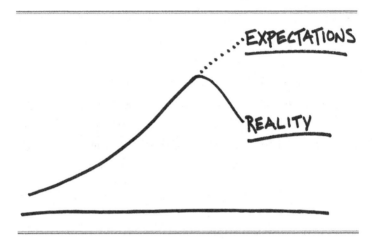

Typically, expectations are based on our recent—often our very recent—experiences. One day, your neighbor's house sells for a big profit. Then your brother's house sells for an even bigger profit. Things have changed. After a while, you adjust your expectations. You now think (assume) that values will continue to rise. And you start to behave differently based on those expectations. Maybe you borrow against your home's rising value and spend the money on a nicer car or a family vacation.

Home prices (and our related behavior) may eventually reach dangerous extremes. At that point, prices may collapse and fall well below any realistic estimate of what homes are worth in the long run. Boom-and-bust cycles often take prices to incredible extremes in both directions. Looking back, it's almost always painfully obvious that we allowed our expectations to get out of whack. At the time, though . . . things are not so clear.

It's important to avoid getting caught up in these cycles. One way to avoid them is to *lengthen our definition of the past.*

History is so important. It has been said that the three most important words in the English language are "remember, remember, remember."

More specifically, we need to think back past the trends of the very recent past, and remember those times in our lives when things changed in ways that really surprised us.

We don't have to look to ancient history for useful examples. Most of us can remember the end of the boom in technology start-ups a decade ago . . . the end of the housing boom . . . the 2008 debt crisis that sent world markets plummeting . . .

You'd think such events would be easy to recall. But we sometimes push such memories aside—especially when things are going well. Truth is, we *like* the new trend. When home prices were rising, we were really happy about it. Why worry about the past when the present is so pleasant?

Because, as the historian and philosopher George Santayana said (more or less), those who don't remember the past just get hammered again and again.

A Little Experience Can Be a Dangerous Thing

When we ignore history, we end up basing our actions on our own limited experience. That can be very dangerous.

I was pretty careful the first time I climbed the Grand Teton. Like most climbers, my partner and I hiked up into the mountains and spent the night so we could rise early and head for the summit before dawn. Everyone said we should get up to the top as early as possible, and head down by ten o'clock in the morning; that way, we'd avoid afternoon thunderstorms.

It was a beautiful day: warm, sunny, almost no wind. We ended up taking a nap on the summit in shorts and T-shirts. We headed down around noon. No worries.

Based on that experience, I took a different approach the next time I set out to climb the peak, this time with a party that included my dad. I wasn't as worried about getting up and down early. We got a late start . . . and we ran into cloudy weather. There was snow on the route. On the summit, we hit an electrical storm. We felt our hair stand up, and we could hear our metal ice axes buzzing. My dad got knocked down by lightning strikes—not once, but twice.

It turns out that there is a reason climbers like to get off the summit of the Grand Teton early. Thunderstorms are common on the summit of the peak in August. We were like tourists who visit Seattle on a sunny day and decide that all those stories about how much it rains are just a myth designed by the locals to keep people from moving there.

Many investors now approaching retirement came of age back at the beginning of the greatest bull market in history—which began almost thirty years ago. They figured investing was easy. So they took on more and more risk. Then the clouds rolled in.

Mountains are dangerous. That doesn't mean you don't go climbing (although *maybe* you don't). But it does mean that if you want to stay alive you'd better respect those dangers.

The same is true of stocks. They're dangerous. When we pretend otherwise, we get into trouble.

Pick Your Poison

We often treat fear and greed—the primary drivers of most of the big behavioral mistakes investors make—as flip sides of the same coin. But they're really two very different emotions. It's important to figure out which emotion is the bigger issue for you. That knowledge will help you manage your behavior during periods of fear and periods of greed.

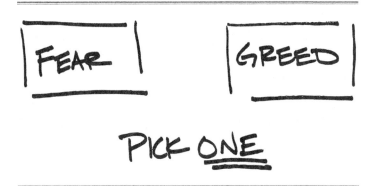

If you're like most people, you will find that the pain of loss outweighs the pleasure you get from gain. In that case, you can manage your portfolio to reduce the pain to a level that you can manage even during truly bad market downturns. That just means being more conservative with your investments. You may miss out on some gains when the market rises—but you'll know that your risk is reasonable.

But what if you have the opposite problem? What if you just can't stand sitting on the investment sidelines and hitting singles and doubles while your brother-in-law brags about hitting home runs? Then you need to tilt your portfolio toward investments that will get you your share of gains when greed is rampant on Wall Street.

If you pursue this more aggressive investment strategy, you will always be positioned for bull markets. But you'll suffer the brunt of the next downturn. That's fine—just make sure the portfolio isn't so aggressive that you can't handle those times.

What I'm saying here is that you can't have it both ways. Building an investment strategy that leans toward managing fear is fine. Building a strategy that leans toward managing greed is also fine. Each path has its benefits and its penalties. The idea is to aim for a balance that truly reflects your own emotional strengths and weaknesses—so that you won't feel compelled to jump in and out of the stock market, shifting back and forth between a more aggressive (managing greed) and a more conservative (managing fear) approach.

I repeat: you can't have it both ways.

And yet we try to do that all the time. When the market soars or hits a rough patch, there's a natural tendency to do something. Fast. Our natural reaction is to sell after bad news (when the market is already down) and buy when news is good (after the market is already up), thus indulging our fear *and* our greed.

It's an impossible strategy.

Overconfidence

Overconfidence is a very serious problem. If you don't think it affects you, that's probably because you're overconfident.

In fact, the people who are most overconfident are the ones least likely to recognize it.

Worse, as the level of overconfidence increases, the cost of our mistakes increases as well, since our confidence makes us willing to take on more and more risk.

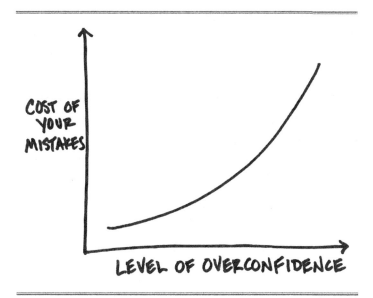

Long-Term Capital Management was a hedge fund run by extremely smart people (Nobel Prize winners, in fact). The geniuses at Long-Term were positive that the most they could ever lose in a single day was $35 million. Then one day in 1998 they lost $553 million. The fund ended up losing $3 billion.

Alan Greenspan, chairman of the Federal Reserve System under four presidents and the subject of countless raves in the financial press, could do no wrong. Yet Mr. Greenspan's steadfast belief in the validity of the models he had used for almost forty years contributed to the worst market crash since the Great Depression. In October 2008, Mr. Greenspan admitted to Congress that he was "shocked" when the models he had used so confidently turned out to be flawed.

It would be nice if only Nobel Prize winners and Federal Reserve Board chairmen were prone to overconfidence—but reams of research show that the rest of us have a similar problem. Fortunately, we can do something about it.

We can recognize that we're not as smart as we think we are. In fact, the smartest investors are the ones who acknowledge that they're *not* smart enough to forecast events or pick the best stock or avoid every scam or . . .

The next time you're about to make an investment decision because you're sure you're right, take the time to have what I call the OC (Overconfidence Conversation). It's been a truly powerful tool to help people in their decisions. Find a friend, spouse, partner, or anyone you trust, and walk them through your answers to the following questions:

- *If I make this change and I am right, what impact will it have on my life?*

- *What impact will it have if I'm wrong?*

- *Have I been wrong before?*

A guy I know had his money invested in his company's stock. He had enough money to retire comfortably, but he believed there was a good chance the value of the stock could continue to rise—maybe even double. He wanted to know if he should sell the stock upon retirement, or hang on and wait for the stock to go up further.

We had the Overconfidence Conversation.

I asked him three questions and we answered them together.

Question one: What happens if you hold the stock and you're right—the stock doubles? Answer: You'll have more money.

Question two: What if you hold the stock and you're wrong? Answer: You're going back to work—maybe for twenty years.

Question three: Have you been wrong before? Answer: Yes.

He sold the stock.

Greater Fools and Your Money

Let's go back again to the late nineties, when people were taking cash out of their homes to buy technology stocks.

That buying frenzy was not based on in-depth analysis, and it continued for so long simply because the market seemed to go nowhere but up. It didn't make any sense. In fact, it was dumb.

Many investors in technology stocks knew the shares they bought were hugely overvalued—but they bought them anyway. Why? Because they figured they would find some idiot (the Greater Fool of stock market lore), and sell the stock to him at an even more ridiculous price.

But what happens when we run out of Greater Fools?

I'm reminded of Warren Buffet, who once said that when the tide goes out, we find out who was swimming naked.

Before you invest your hard-earned money, ask yourself: Are you buying a particular investment because you think it's a good investment? Or are you relying on a Greater Fool to come along? If so, doesn't that make you—no offense—a bit foolish yourself?

A Losing Pattern

One day I was reading the paper, and I came across the weekly survey of investor sentiment done by the American Association of Individual Investors. This survey reported that investors hadn't been so bullish since the market peak some months earlier.

Hmmm. I seemed to recall that the same survey just two weeks earlier had found that investors were more *bearish* than they had been in more than a year.

What had changed in two weeks? The only thing I knew for sure was that the market was up 5 percent between the time investors wanted to sell and the time they wanted to buy.

It was the usual insanity.

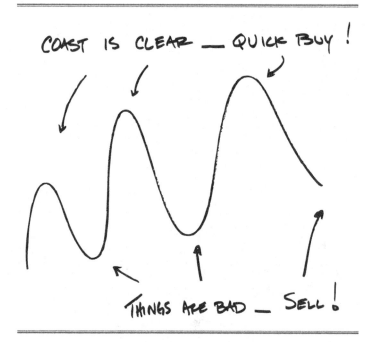

COAST IS CLEAR — QUICK BUY!

THINGS ARE BAD — SELL!

Once again, people were excited about buying stocks because stocks had just become more expensive.

Sigh. We've been doing this for a long time. We do it because we make investing decisions based on *how we feel* rather than *what we know.* Falling stocks scare us; rising stocks attract us. But we know buying high and selling low leads to losses—and we need to stop doing that if we want to get different results.

Can we stop, though? Some of us can. But many of us can't help ourselves. We are going to continue to run away from stocks when they cause us pain.

If you find yourself routinely buying or selling at the

wrong time, it's time to do something different. One alternative—admittedly a pretty drastic one—is to swear off the stock market forever.

I'm not kidding. If you can't stand the heat (and the record clearly shows that most people can't) then maybe you should have the sense to get out of the kitchen. Whatever the experts may claim, steering clear of stocks isn't stupid. You'll just be following Will Rogers's advice: focus on the return *of* your money instead of the return *on* your money.

Of course, if you avoid stocks altogether, you will be giving up some potential returns. You will need to compensate by saving more or adjusting your goals.

That would be better than continuing to buy high and sell low.

But maybe there's an even better alternative. Maybe you should get help from a financial professional you really trust, who will help you make better decisions. Sometimes we just need someone to walk us in off the ledge when we're about to do something dumb.

Even if you get trustworthy professional help, you need to stay involved in the process. This is what the process should look like:

- **Have a real plan.** I am not talking about one of those two-inch-thick books we've come to know as financial plans. I'm talking about deciding where you are today, where you want to be later, and how you will behave in order to get there.

- **Find investments to populate your plan.** This comes at the *end* of the planning process, *after* you've established your goals and put together a road map to reach them. You would never spend time researching and debating whether to travel by plane, train, or car until you figured out where you were going.

- **Admit there is a problem.** The first step to quitting a destructive habit is to admit that you have a problem in the first place. Reviewing past decisions will help. Did you get caught up in the tech bubble in 1999? How about real estate in 2006? Did you sell stocks in 2002, late 2008, or early 2009?

- **Face the fact that cash is not a solution to a crisis.** Going to cash until things "clear up" is like jumping out of the frying pan into the fire. Normally, people go to cash to alleviate their stress: they just can't handle the pain anymore. But when you sell you have a new problem: when to get back in. The most common "solution" to that problem is to buy back in when things have "cleared up." Of course, when things have "cleared up," the market will be higher. So what we're talking about is engaging in a plan to sell low (now) and buy high (later) on purpose. That's a bad plan.

- **Develop a checklist of questions to ask before you make major financial decisions.** How are you feeling? Are you acting out of fear or greed—or do you have a clear take on what's going on? Are you reacting to the media? Are you doing this because other people are doing it? Are those people good role models? Does this decision flow naturally out of your plan and support your goals? This checklist approach works for pilots and doctors. Likewise, it will help you avoid mistakes in investment behavior.

- **Take your time.** Try writing down any proposed change in your investment portfolio and then let it sit for twenty-four hours. Maybe call a trusted friend or advisor and walk them through your thinking before you make the change. Often just hearing yourself will convince you to forget the whole thing.

- **Incorporate new information slowly.** You can learn things during market corrections, and what you learn may have implications for your strategy and your goals. During the decline of 2008 to 2009, many of us learned that risk is not simply an abstract concept. That experience might have led you to scale back your goals. That would be a reason to make a change to your investments—perhaps becoming less aggressive. But take your time. Wait until things settle down and you can think rationally about the next course of action.

- **Focus on your own behavior, not the market's behavior.** "Have you seen what the market is doing?" People often say this when they are in a state of shock or exhilaration. They're ready to go to cash until things "clear up," or they're preparing to load up on stocks before it's "too late." Notice the implication that the market is "doing" something right now. In reality, we only know what the market has already done. It may be peaking or bottoming out and ready to reverse course.

We don't know what comes next for the financial markets. In the end, our own behavior is all that we can control—and ultimately, our behavior can make a huge difference in our financial success and our personal happiness.

In other words, it's up to us to close the behavior gap.

THE PERFECT INVESTMENT

NOT long ago, I came across a story about a hedge fund manager who was buying up the world's chocolate supply. The story got me thinking about the craziness of the global markets. How are we supposed to understand them when a hedge fund manager in London, with offices in West Africa, is buying chocolate on exchanges all over the world and maybe (who knows?) blowing my wife's chocolate budget right here in Park City, Utah?

COCOA FUTURES   MEAN OLD HEDGE FUND MANAGER

THERE GOES THE CHOCOLATE BUDGET

And yet some investors might take the news about the hedge fund manager buying up chocolate as a signal to go out and load up on chocolate futures (yes, there are such things). Probably not the best idea, given how many factors affect the price of chocolate, and given the fact that we don't know the hedge fund manager from Adam. For all we know he could be a nut case. Or maybe he is buying chocolate because he really, really likes chocolate. Or maybe he thinks chocolate is a hedge against another recession (don't people eat a lot of chocolate in a recession?).

Chocolate futures may be the perfect investment. But I don't know enough about chocolate or about that hedge fund manager or his motives to decide if chocolate is a good investment. So maybe I'll just go eat a candy bar and forget about it.

Finding Your Financial Balance

Planning for your financial future is about making trade-offs. It's largely a question of dealing with the constant tension between living for today and saving for some future event.

What seems like a complicated process (so much so that we often give up before we even start) is really just a balancing act. I've found that it helps to put a framework around this process, which we can do by asking a few questions:

- How much can you reasonably save?

- What rate of return will you earn?

- How much do you need?

- And when will you need it?

While these questions may sound simple, they're not necessarily easy to answer. And certainly there are more questions that you can ask. But these four are pretty central.

Only one of the questions—the second one—has to do

with investments. Yet so much of our anxiety about money revolves around that projected rate of return.

Rate of return is only one relatively small part of the equation. The pursuit of higher investment returns may make a positive difference in our outlook, assuming things go as we hope. But there are other things you can do that are more certain—you don't have to rely on hope—and just as effective. Save a little more if you can. Consider retiring a little later or pursuing a second career.

Planning for your financial future is a balancing act rather than a single-minded pursuit of the highest return. Real planning requires thought, frequent course corrections, and, above all, an effort to keep things in balance. Finding that balance is a different process for everyone.

In Search of the World's Best Investment

People spend a lot of time and energy trying to find the "best" stocks, mutual funds, or other investments. Magazines devote covers to this search, and authors write books about it. There are entire industries built around this wild goose chase.

But let's clear this up right now: there is no such thing as the best investment.

This widespread notion that somewhere there exists an investment that outshines all others simply doesn't make sense. No single investment is right for everyone. The best investments for you depend on personal factors—your goals, your personality, your existing holdings, your credit card balance . . . The list is endless.

Financial products—including things like bank accounts and insurance policies as well as investments—should be judged on how well they help you reach your goals. Since your goals are unique, what might be right for you could be a disaster for someone else.

Moreover, the specific investments you choose probably won't determine your financial prospects. I often run into folks who spend a lot of time hunting for great investments even as they ignore more fundamental issues in their financial situation.

Someone might come in looking for the next hot stock. I ask a few questions, and find out that they have no life or disability insurance. Or a new client will come into my office looking for the highest-yielding savings account, while carrying a credit card balance at 18 percent interest. That's my cue to say something like this: *What are we doing scraping around for an extra half percent in CD yields? How about if we use some of your savings to pay off some credit card debt—which is pretty much like earning an 18 percent yield?*

I have a friend who retired from his job as a doctor and became a financial advisor. Clients who focus on the highest returns while ignoring bigger problems in their finances remind him of one of his former patients, a smoker with high blood pressure.

This patient would come in and ask my friend which blood pressure medication would work best in his case, and then debate the question endlessly.

My friend couldn't believe it. He had fantasies of reading the guy the riot act. His imagined monologue went something like this:

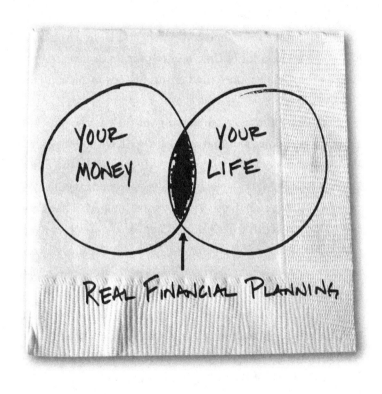

But you still smoke! Why are we having these endless debates about different medications when YOU STILL SMOKE! It almost doesn't matter which medication we choose—and in any case, you have no idea what you're talking about! You're not a doctor!

The smoker should quit smoking. That is something that matters, and it's a decision entirely within his power. Likewise, the guy with the expensive credit card debt should stop watching CNBC and find a way to pay that balance off—and earn an immediate, guaranteed 18 percent return on that investment. The guy without life insurance should get some and protect his family, rather than waste time reading cover stories about hot stocks. Searching for the perfect investment can distract you from more important things. And, by the way, it doesn't work.

(Don't) Collect Them All!

Think of each investment that you own as a thread in a tapestry. Each component of a portfolio should be there for a reason—and not because you think it's a candidate for world's best investment.

Some people collect investments like kids used to collect baseball cards. This year they buy the mutual funds they read about in *Smart Money* magazine. Next year they buy the top ten funds recommended by *Money* magazine. A year later they buy two or three new international funds that showed up on the home page of Forbes.com.

Before they know it, these collectors have a smorgasbord of unrelated investments, with no cohesive strategy at work.

Worse, those investments often are concentrated in sim-

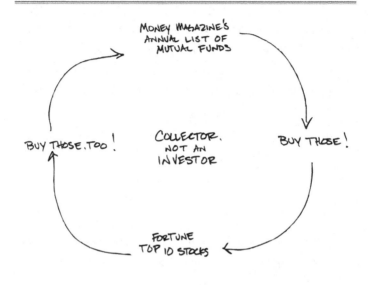

ilar types of assets—maybe large company stocks or long-term bonds—just as a baseball card collector might focus on the Boston Red Sox. I often meet people who believe they're properly diversified because they own fifteen or twenty mutual funds. But different funds can have very similar investment strategies. And when the value of one fund falls, the shares of funds with similar strategies will fall as well.

Meanwhile, there are costs involved in maintaining such a smorgasbord of holdings, not to mention the time and trouble it takes to keep track of them all.

Remember, you're not a collector. You're an investor. You want investments that work together to close the gap between you and your financial goals. You also need to make sure that what you own doesn't expose you to more risk than you can handle.

The financial magazines on your coffee table are kind of like your dentist or your brother-in-law. They may play a constructive role in your life. But they don't know which investments are best—let alone best for you.

Looking for Mr. Lynch

Whenever a mutual fund advertises performance, the Securities and Exchange Commission requires that it include the disclaimer that "a fund's past performance does not necessarily predict future results."

A study by researchers at Arizona State University and Wake Forest School of Law suggests that this warning is not enough. The researchers recommend something a bit stronger: "Do not expect the fund's quoted past performance to continue in the future. [Our s]tudies show that mutual funds that have outperformed their peers in the past generally do not outperform them in the future. Strong past performance is often a matter of chance."

Despite the SEC warning and pretty conclusive evidence that past performance has very little predictive value, most of us still use performance as the predominant factor in choosing our investments.

This is one of those times in investing when our experience in other areas of life works against us. When you are considering hiring a contractor to remodel your house, one of the first things you do is look at the contractor's work on

other houses. It seems reasonable to expect that their work on your house will be that good, if not better.

When it comes to mutual funds, however, the past has almost no predictive value. People have spent years looking for a way to identify mutual funds that will do well in the future. They have looked at education, experience, and, of course, past performance.

It turns out that fees are the only factor that reliably predicts a fund's performance. The higher the expense ratio —the cost of owning the fund—the worse the performance for shareholders. This is a case where you actually get what you *don't* pay for.

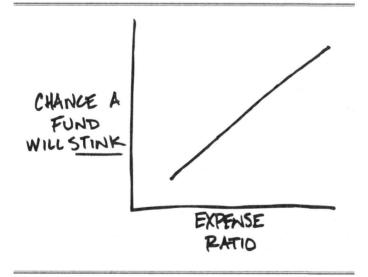

CHANCE A FUND WILL STINK

EXPENSE RATIO

Despite this, we still scour media lists of "Ten Hot Funds to Own Now" (which are typically based on past performance), looking for places to put our savings.

One of my financial writer friends once wrote a magazine cover story about finding the next Peter Lynch (the legendary manager of Fidelity's Magellan Fund from 1977 to 1990). Lynch had just retired, to the shock of many fund investors, and people were looking for a successor. My friend ended up profiling likely candidates—folks who had delivered very strong returns over five years or longer.

Those managers turned out to be a decent bunch, on the whole. One or two were quite successful; one or two flopped; the others were average. Not a bad bunch, but no legends in sight.

Trying to figure out which fund will lead the pack during the next quarter or next year or next decade is a fool's game. Focus instead on finding a low-cost investment that you can stick with over the long haul.

The Next Apple? Don't Bite.

The odds of you picking the next hot stock like Google or Apple are insanely low. Yet, like those misleading lottery advertisements, popular stories about the next "big" investment tempt us to believe that we can do it.

A few years after my friend tried (and failed) to find the next Peter Lynch, he wrote a story called something like "Finding the Next Microsoft." The story was fun to write—he and his team of reporters interviewed dozens of top money managers and analysts to try to understand what made Microsoft such a find in its day. Then they went looking for other stocks that had similar characteristics. It was a cool exercise, and my friend learned a lot, but he didn't find the next Microsoft. The article got nominated for a national

award—it was meticulously reported, and a lot of fun to read—but my friend can't even remember the names of the stocks he named in the piece.

He eventually quit writing stock-picking stories. "It's a little like writing about horse racing," he says. "It's really fun, and you learn a lot about how companies operate and how people try to value stocks. Sometimes you can help weed out the worst stocks, and once in a while you come across something that works out and you think it's because you're so smart. But in the end most of it is just entertainment. You know that, and you hope no one takes it too seriously. But you know some people do."

Looking for the next hot stock is bad enough. Investing in today's hot stock is even worse.

Nathan Pinger at YCharts, an organization that analyzes

market data, notes that Google's stock price rose from $100 to $600 per share from August 2004 to December 2010. Apple climbed more than 4,000 percent from the end of 2000 to the end of 2010. As a result, lots of people have decided those are stocks that belong in their portfolios. Unfortunately, Pinger adds a footnote: "Trying to pick a stock's future growth path based on past growth is like trying to guess if a coin will come up heads or tails when you know that the last toss was a heads. The previous toss tells you nothing."

RISK

MARKET VALUE

In fact, that may understate the case against buying top performers. The hotter the investment, the greater the risk. The brother of a friend of a friend of mine bought a bunch of silver in 2010 and made a lot of money—maybe $200,000. It was a risky investment, and it worked. So he decided to buy more. He figured if silver was a bargain at his original price, it must be an even better bargain at triple that price.

We don't know how this guy's investment will end up. But does his behavior make sense to you? It made sense to him! After all, he read a bunch of articles saying silver's price was going to keep rising!

This reminds me of another problem confronting every investor. We have a tendency to assume that what we do know is more important than what we don't know. This silver fan had read a bunch of bullish reports from firms that wanted to sell him silver. It never occurred to him that there might also be lots of reasons *not* to invest in silver. So he put his retirement money into the metal—and suggested that his brother do the same. (If getting investment advice from your brother is a bad idea, giving investment advice to your brother is even worse. In this case the brother said no thanks . . .)

Every so often I'll get a phone call from a client who has his sights set on the next big stock. To him, it makes perfect sense to dump his plan, ignore his goals, and bet the future on, well, a tip from his brother, who had the luck to buy the stock back when it was cheap.

Our willingness to take a flier makes a certain kind of emotional sense. We grow up hoping and kind of believing that superheroes and magic are real. We root for underdogs even though we know beating the favorite will take a miracle. We even buy lottery tickets. It just doesn't feel all that crazy to believe that the stars will align and one financial decision will change our lives forever. In fact, it feels good.

The problem is that when you chase after a particular

investment, you lose sight of the things that actually matter, like your goals and plans.

Fantasies are only fun while they last. Back in late 1999, I was resisting the temptation to buy technology stocks—a temptation that was growing more and more powerful by the month. Everyone—my friends, my family, my clients— wanted me to buy technology stocks. It didn't help that my brother-in-law works in the technology industry, and he kept telling me stories about people making easy money.

And you know what? I gave in! I went and found the hottest technology stock I could find (InfoSpace) and I made a pretty hefty investment in it.

The stock price went from below $100 to over $1300 in a matter of months, but by March 2001, the stock had dropped below $25.

That's how it goes. The terrible irony in all this is that the people who are trying the hardest to stick to their plans—the ones who hold out the longest before they finally capitulate—are the ones who end up getting hurt the worst because they buy nearest the peak. Once those hard-core holdouts give in, you know the top can't be far away, because there is no one left to buy.

If you drop by my office, you will notice a framed stock certificate on the wall. Look closely: those are my InfoSpace shares. I had the certificate mailed to me so I could frame it and look at it every day, as a reminder of my folly. It stung at the time—still stings a bit—but the lesson was worth the loss.

For 99.99 percent of us, chasing after the Googles and the Apples of the world will lead to disappointment.

Meanwhile, the odds of achieving financial success are much higher if we simply work, save, and build an investment portfolio based on reality.

Investing Isn't Always Fair

Of course, not all investing stories have a clear and uplifting moral. Sometimes folly is rewarded, and good sense and prudence are punished—at least in the short run. That is why I judge investment advice not by its outcome but by the validity of the principle it's based upon.

One client came to me with the shares of his grandmother's mining company. The family had lost millions of dollars trying to save the firm, which played a large role in the family lore. The stock had sunk to around two dollars. The client was trying to decide what to do. He was worried that if he sold the stock, it might recover—and then he and his family would wish they had kept it.

I told him if he sold the stock and it doubled or tripled—which was a real possibility—he'd feel badly. But I also told him that if he kept the stock, it might go to zero—and then he'd feel much, much worse.

When making good investment decisions, it helps to be emotionally prepared for a painful result. But you need to keep making good decisions anyway. In the end, that's a better strategy than making bad decisions.

I'm reminded of that guy from England, thirty-two years old, who sold everything he owned and took the cash ($135,300) to Vegas for one roll of the roulette wheel.

Good decision or bad?

Turns out he won—doubling his money.

Now, was that a good decision or a bad one?

Answer: it was still a horrible decision.

Another client came to see me after his employer merged with another firm. He was forced to retire early, but he took with him a great big pile of stock in the newly merged company. The stock amounted to 90 percent of his net worth. He had been devoted to his former employer, and being forced to retire was traumatic for him.

Now I was also telling him to sell the stock, his last connection to the firm.

Client: *Why? Do you think the stock price is going down?*

Me: *No. My advice has nothing to do with the stock's price or where I think it's going. I don't know where it's going, so it doesn't matter what I think anyway.*

Client: *But what if the stock goes up?*

Me: *You'll feel bad. But it doesn't matter. Holding 90 percent of your net worth in one stock is a terrible idea.*

My point was that decisions should be based on principles, not on our feelings about what's going to happen. The principle here was the one that says it's always a bad idea to have too much of your net worth wrapped up in a single investment, let alone a single stock.

He sold it. The stock declined by more than 90 percent. He still calls me Santa Claus. I keep reminding him that selling his stock would have been a good decision even if the stock had immediately doubled.

There is no best investment out there. But sometimes, the best *decision* is obvious.

IGNORE ADVICE,
MAKE FUN OF FORECASTS

THE BEHAVIOR GAP

WE all like giving advice. It makes us feel needed, useful, important. But let's face it: most of the advice we give (and get) is useless or worse.

A friend of mine and his wife recently built a small house on a pretty remote beach in Central America. They went down for a few months, and the neighbors all dropped by. Each neighbor had a different piece of advice, usually in the form of a warning. One neighbor had suffered from termites. He predicted that my friend's house would be eaten up by the bugs, while offering various ideas about how to prevent this. Another neighbor had been robbed. She offered dire warnings about that, with lots of advice about security measures. Another neighbor was terrified of lightning, which had struck a tree in her yard, so she warned my friend and his wife to watch out for lightning. Another neighbor had lost his property in a legal battle. He warned my friend about that risk and urged him to think about selling before it was too late.

My friend thought it was all pretty funny. "No doubt something bad will happen to our house at some point," he says. "But it will be something completely different. It will be *our* disaster."

His story got me thinking about the origins of advice. People tend to give you advice that's based on their own fears, their own experience, their own expertise, their own motivations. Their advice typically has little to do with the reality of your life. Even our friends and family, who presumably know us fairly well, usually get it wrong.

Most of the advice we come across in the media (including books!) is even worse. It typically has little or nothing to do with the reality of our lives. How could it, when the person giving the advice doesn't even know us?

Predictions, with their accompanying (explicit or implied) advice about what to do now, are the worst. In 2010, *The New York Times* ran an article called "A Market Forecast That Says 'Take Cover.' " The piece offered advice from an expert who suggested that "individual investors should move completely out of the market and hold cash and cash equivalents, like Treasury bills, for years to come."

The article got lots of attention. It was among the paper's most emailed articles for several days.

But what are you supposed to do with this information? Should you follow the advice to "take cover," regardless of your age, unique goals, and family situation? Come to think of it, where do people get off giving specific investment advice to complete strangers? Would you take advice from a random guy on the street—even if he was wearing a fancy suit? Why take his advice when you read it in a newspaper?

What about the advice handed down via books, television, and other media by popular personal finance gurus? Some of them have great ideas. But does their generic advice apply to you? Maybe. But maybe not.

Take annuities, which can provide a guaranteed monthly income (in exchange for a sizable up-front investment). The best gurus advise their readers to steer clear of them—and generally, they're right. Annuities are in fact a terrible deal for most people, thanks in part to their high fees. I have a bias against the things myself. I've considered using annuities dozens of times, and I can only think of two occasions when I ended up using them. But in those two cases, annuities worked.

One case involved a widow I know who had just enough money to get through retirement. She couldn't afford to take any risks with her capital, but she needed to earn more than CDs paid. After carefully looking at all her options, we decided that her circumstances called for an annuity with a guaranteed rate of return.

This was in 1999. Based on how things worked out, her son still calls me to thank me for keeping her out of the stock market. His words: "If we'd done things differently, she might have ended up out of money and living in our basement."

Again, as a rule of thumb, annuities are not great investments. But my point is that rules of thumb are dangerous, especially when they come from people who don't know you. I'd go so far as to say there are very few rules of thumb that actually apply to any single individual. They're starting points, at best.

As for that famous financial planning personality, he may be a genius. He may have helped a lot of people. But remember: He doesn't know you. He is not *your* financial planner.

Personal Finance Is Personal

Take it from me (a stranger): following the advice of strangers is a tricky business. Let's say you're planning a vacation. You read a magazine article about someone who had a great time at a dude ranch in Montana. The pictures look fantastic. You go—and the bugs drive you crazy and you hate the heat and the food and the horses. Maybe the travel writer actually had a great time. But you're not him.

The financial press, personal finance bloggers, and best-selling authors are all sources of information. They may have good ideas, which you may find useful. But they can't tell you how the information and the ideas apply to your situation. They don't know you. More to the point, they *aren't* you.

My friend Tim Maurer is a financial planner, educator, and author. His favorite line goes like this: "Personal finance . . . is more personal than it is finance."

It's true. Planning for your financial future is personal. It has to be. A good plan will be unique to your situation, and what is right for your situation may be a disaster for your neighbor. So ponder how the advice you encounter applies to you before you make important decisions about your money.

Their Guess, Your Money

One day some years back, a friend came into my office worried about something called "the bin Laden trades." A rumor was going around that a mysterious investor had made a huge bet that the stock market would decline in September 2007. The theory was that one person (maybe Osama bin Laden!) had made the bet because he or she knew about an impending terrorist attack that would hammer stock prices. My friend wondered if he should sell stocks to avoid the coming crash.

Sounded pretty far out. I told my friend to ignore the rumors and the related predictions. As it turned out, there

was no such conspiracy, no such mysterious investor . . . and the projected crash didn't happen.

What's more, even if the rumors had been true, we would have been right to ignore them.

With very few exceptions, market and economic forecasts are really nothing more than guesses—some of them pretty wild. But as we continue to reckon with an uncertain economic future, it is more tempting than ever to seek out a guru. We want someone to tell us what's coming so we can plan accordingly. We like the idea that we can know the future and prepare for it.

It just isn't so.

When you come across forecasts, keep in mind the following:

THE BEHAVIOR GAP

No one knows what the future holds. History doesn't really help except to tell us that it's hard to forecast accurately.

If people make enough guesses, they are bound to get at least a few of them right. Even a broken clock is right twice a day. So don't take it too seriously when someone calls a market turn correctly. Most likely, it's luck.

I came across a story by Joe Keohane in *The Boston Globe.* The piece focused on New York University economist Nouriel Roubini. Back in 2006, Roubini predicted that the economy was about to go off a cliff. When the Great Recession arrived, he was promoted to prophet. But Roubini has made other extreme predictions, and he's often been wrong. To take one example: in March 2009, he predicted the S&P 500 would drop below 600 that year; it closed the year at 1,115, for a 12-month gain of 23.5 percent.

The guys who occasionally nail a very dramatic forecast are actually less reliable than their more middle-of-the-road colleagues. Keohane cites a 2010 study by Oxford economist Jerker Denrell and New York University's Christina Fang, who dug through data from the article "Survey of Economic Forecasts" in *The Wall Street Journal.*

Denrell and Fang concluded that economists who correctly call the most unexpected events have worse long-term records than the rest of the pack. In fact, they noted that the analyst with the largest number and the highest proportion of accurate *extreme* forecasts had by far the worst *overall* forecasting record.

Makes sense when you think about it. The guys who tend to make bold forecasts tend to be wrong—because they're constantly out on a limb. Once in a while they're right, and then they look like geniuses. More often, they're just out there in left field.

If you nail a big guess as a market forecaster, you can live off it for a long time. Think of all the people who came out of the woodwork claiming to have forecast the collapse of 2008. Most of them were just lucky.

Thoughtful economists and market analysts can provide useful insight into the present. But they can't predict the future.

No one can.

Gurus Are Right Until They're Wrong

In July 2010, well-known market forecaster Robert Prechter (who champions something called the Elliott Wave Principle) made this prediction: "The Dow, which now stands at 9,686.48, is likely to fall well below 1,000 over perhaps five or six years as a grand market cycle comes to an end."

Early in 2011, Yale's Robert Shiller predicted that the Standard & Poor's 500-stock index would rise from 1,280 (its level on January 10, 2011) to 1,430 over the next decade, a 1.3 percent increase per year.

In January 2011, veteran market watcher Laszlo Birinyi forecast that the S&P would hit 2,854 by (mark the date) the end of the day on September 4, 2013.

So there you have it. Three market gurus with three divergent forecasts, all pretty extreme. All three forecasts showed up in reputable, mainstream news outlets.

What's an investor to think or do?

Ignore them.

A GUESS BY SOME GURU + YOUR $ = WHO KNOWS !

It can be fun to chat with friends or colleagues about your opinion of the stock market. Sometimes it can feel like the duty of any self-respecting American to have an opinion about the market and the economy.

But no one can tell you where the stock market (or any market) is going.

And even if someone did possess that ability, how could you (or I) distinguish that person from the clowns who get lucky once in a while? Would you listen to Prechter, Shiller, Birinyi . . . or someone else?

So Why Do We Listen?

We get interested in predictions because we're human. A number of factors conspire to make us easy marks for forecasters.

For one thing, our survival instinct means that we're constantly trying to predict what danger may be lurking in the bushes. And since we're social animals, we love being in the know. We love being the one to break the news on Facebook or Twitter. On a primal level, we want to be the (highly valued) person who warns others of danger or offers them useful information.

Meanwhile, it's scary to accept that much of what goes on is random and that the only constant seems to be change. We rely on predicting and forecasting for almost every decision we make, including the weather, our commute time, and even what to wear. It makes us anxious to admit that most predictions (our own and those of others) are flawed, at best. And so we are grateful when people—especially famous, respected people quoted in mainstream publications—offer to tell us what will happen in the future.

Okay. So it may feel kind of scary to give up the idea that you can rely on strangers to tell you what to do with your money or what's going to happen next in the financial markets. In fact, however, giving up those notions is the first step toward a certain kind of freedom.

Our continued willingness to listen to advice and predictions, despite experience and research that suggest they can't help us, is an example of why it's so difficult to behave correctly when it comes to our relationship with investments. We want someone to tell us what to do. But in the end, we have to recognize that the future is unpredictable. Advice and forecasts are often distractions from our real task: getting to know ourselves and our goals, making choices aligned with those goals, and adapting to the surprises that are bound to come along.

We have evolved to scan the horizon for data, and make quick snap judgments. Andrew Lo, a finance professor at MIT, notes that if you were to go into your closet each day and try to come up with the perfect combination of clothes, you would have to choose from thousands of possible combinations.

The same is true for investments. There are millions of ways to design your financial life. So it's nice to imagine that someone will tell us what to do—or give us information that will make our choices very simple (*stocks are going up; buy stocks*).

So what do we do when we realize that advice is generic and predictions are unreliable? Isn't that a big problem? Not really. We don't have to pick the perfect investments, or the perfect portfolio.

After all, we don't need or want someone to pick our clothes for us each morning based on predictions about what our day will be like or who we'll encounter and what they'll think of our pink shirt. Instead, we rely on our experience and our judgment and our own taste in clothing.

We also rely on our flexibility—if we get it wrong, we'll adapt. If it's hotter than we expected, we'll take off our jacket. If we're underdressed, we'll apologize. No big deal. And meanwhile, if we need someone else's perspective, we can always ask: *How do I look?*

Likewise, we can design our portfolios to suit our best current understanding of how financial markets tend to work, and what we want to achieve over the coming years. When things change, we can adapt.

And if we need perspective, we can turn to trustworthy people who know us—not some stranger with a show on cable.

You Gotta Be You

A few years ago, I had a discussion with somebody who was unhappy with the results of his investing strategy. We discussed one way he could do it differently and he asked me, "If that is such a good idea, why doesn't Harvard do it that way?"

I wasn't totally surprised by the question. The guy is a professor, and at the time Harvard and Yale were getting a lot of press for the investment performance of their endowments.

Anyway, I told him I didn't actually know what Harvard and Yale were doing with their portfolios (I had a rough idea, but none of the details). More to the point, their goals as educational institutions were almost certainly very different from his goals as a human being.

Harvard's goals might reflect everything from the size of their current holdings to their decision to build a new campus in, say, Ecuador.

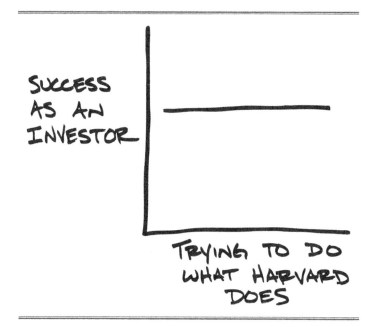

The investing goals of an individual or family will be more along the lines of educating your kids (maybe at Harvard!) or helping your elderly parents remain financially independent.

Institutions also get very different deals on their investments. Fees on alternative investments and hedging strategies put them out of the reach of people like you and me. Endowments get a break because they can invest large amounts. As a result, they may rely heavily on those tools.

In short, your portfolio is not a university endowment. Expecting that the same investing strategies will work for you is a little bit like shopping at a big and tall store if you're only five feet six. It isn't a good fit.

Okay, so maybe it never occurred to you to invest like the guys at Harvard and Yale—or, for that matter, your own state university. But you've probably been tempted to follow the strategies of other successful investors.

Sometimes they're friends and family. Often they're famous money managers with best-selling books. But the same lesson applies: They have different-size portfolios, different goals, and different risk tolerances. They may have something to teach you, but you need a strategy that's made specifically for you.

Some of us know better than to take financial advice from family members—almost always a terrible idea. But what about Warren Buffett, the Oracle of Omaha? Everyone agrees that he is a brilliant investor, and that his approach makes a lot of sense. But his approach suits his personality and his goals and the goals of his shareholders at Berkshire Hathaway.

Here's a guy who has always loved investing—it's his meat and drink, along with Cherry Coke (ugh!). He studied with Benjamin Graham, the father of modern securities analysis, and went on to invent a version of value investing based on finding, acquiring, and managing great businesses—which is really a full-time job, even if you are a genius. Buffett gets a break on many of his acquisitions, because other big players want him, not someone else, as a partner.

Does any of that sound like something you or I can duplicate?

Meanwhile, Buffett is trying to build a business himself, delivering long-term value to shareholders who have their own agendas. It's all pretty complicated, and occasionally even he gets it wildly wrong.

Maybe we can learn a few general principles from Buffet. But most of us are not going to invest like Buffett, no matter how many books we read.

I hate to break it to you: You're not Warren Buffett. You're not even the next Warren Buffett. Fortunately, you don't have to be.

You can be you.

~~FINANCIAL~~ LIFE PLANNING

I spend a lot of time talking and writing about worst-case scenarios: investors behaving badly, people losing their retirement, and so on.

But let's not forget why we're so focused on our financial security. We want to be happy, and to provide a good life for our loved ones.

This sketch is one of my favorites, even though it doesn't say a word about money. When I get up in the morning, I try to remember what really makes me happy—great experiences with the people I love. When I use that goal as the baseline for my decision-making, it becomes a lot easier to focus on the things that really matter when it comes to investing: things like working hard, saving a lot, and behaving wisely.

What Money Buys

Happiness is more about expectations and desire than it is about income. A friend just back from an extended trip to Nepal was struck by how little people over there had and how happy they seemed. She was only there a few weeks, and poverty is a real problem in Nepal; it causes much suffering. But still, some of those folks seemed pretty happy to my friend.

A recent study by Daniel Kahneman, a winner of the Nobel Prize in Economic Sciences, and Princeton professor Angus Deaton found that Americans report an increase in happiness as their incomes rise to $75,000 a year. After that, the impact of rising income on happiness levels off.

Makes sense. Most of us find that it's pretty hard to be happy when we can't afford food, shelter, or health care—and it helps to add hobbies and a social life and maybe even some travel. Once we have those things, we can afford to turn our attention to deeper needs (love, personal growth)—the sort of needs that money may not address.

Where does that leave us? Well, most of us need at least some money to have a shot at happiness. Beyond that, money can be a tool that helps us pursue the things that will bring us happiness—but it can't tell us what those things might be.

All of this means that we have to decide what will make us happy, and then make financial decisions that support those goals. If we want community and shared purpose, we might go work for a nonprofit foundation and give up the bigger bucks in the private sector. Is that a good financial decision or a bad financial decision? The question doesn't make sense: it's not a financial decision.

It's a *life* decision.

Financial decisions almost always are life decisions. Before you decide on your financial goals, you need to choose your life goals.

When you link financial decisions to life decisions, you encounter a whole different set of challenges. Each person's financial situation becomes unique, because their goals are unique. It's no longer about abstractions like a secure retirement or a college education—it's about *your* vision of retirement, and *your* child*'s* education. What brings you happiness may not bring your neighbor happiness—and a canned plan won't work for either one of you.

We all know this on some level, and yet we continue to act as if the connection between money and income were simple—as if more money will always make us happier. Even (or is it especially?) rich people act this way.

I'm not foolish enough to believe that money plays no role in happiness. Money can certainly relieve stress, and reduced stress can certainly lead to increased happiness. So there is some correlation, but it seems pretty fuzzy to me.

I wonder if linking happiness to money might be part of this continuing obsession we seem to have with measuring, comparing, and competing. As far as I can tell there is no unit of "happy." We have no standard quantitative way to measure it. But if we link happiness to money, that is something we all understand. It gives me a way to compare my level of happiness to yours.

Unfortunately, the more we try to define, measure, and compete for happiness, the harder it is to find.

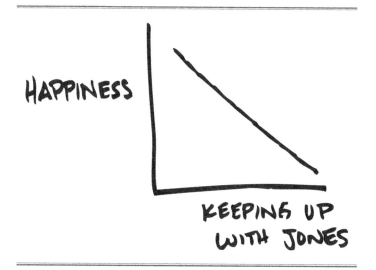

Even so, we continue to compare our lot in life with the guy standing next to us. We measure our happiness based on whether we're keeping up with the Joneses. And we end up less happy for it.

Okay. So what's the connection, if there is any, between happiness and money?

First, money can buy happiness—up to a point. You need some money to be happy, but once the basics are covered the link fades quickly.

Second, experiences matter more than objects. Remember the thrill of finally getting the shiny new toy? At some point, it stopped being new and shiny. The same doesn't apply to that amazing trip you took with your family. The trip may last for only a few days, but the memories you create

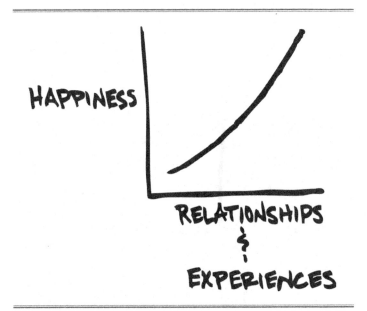

will bring you greater happiness throughout your life than the gadget you picked up at the store last week.

Third, happiness sneaks up on you when you let it. We may have an inalienable right to pursue happiness, but there's no guarantee that we'll actually capture it. Maybe we've let ourselves get so caught up in the pursuit that we're missing the point.

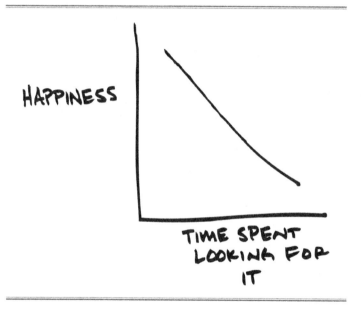

When the Zen master Wu Li was asked what to do to achieve enlightenment, he responded, "Chop wood, carry water."

When he was asked what to do when you have achieved enlightenment, he responded, "Chop wood, carry water."

Maybe happiness comes easiest when we are so busy

working, taking care of kids, shoveling snow, or cleaning the house that we forget to look for it.

Love or Money?

Instead of spending time searching for the best financial product, we should reflect on what is really important to us and then align our use of capital with those values. Rather than reading the latest list of "The Ten Best Investments for a Post-Credit-Crisis World," spend some time thinking about what is really important to you.

Maybe start with this question: what makes you happy?

David Brooks, author and *New York Times* columnist, wrote an interesting column after Sandra Bullock won her Academy Award for best actress. You may recall that around the same time, she found out that her husband was cheating on her.

Brooks asked his readers: Would you take that as a deal? A huge professional success, followed by the collapse of a key personal relationship?

You probably won't be shocked to find out that marital happiness trumps professional success as a predictor of personal happiness.

Likewise, Brooks pointed out, the connection between income and happiness is pretty complex—and not as strong as you might expect. As we've seen, once you hit the middle class, it doesn't much matter how much more you make.

By contrast, personal relationships are absolutely crucial to happiness. Brooks noted that joining a group that meets once a month produces as much happiness as doubling your income. (Wow!) Just being married is (on average) worth $100,000 a year in terms of emotional gains.

Brooks's conclusion: modern society concentrates on the wrong things. Governments track economic trends, but pay little attention to how social programs and institutions affect happiness. Likewise, individuals worry too much about money and not enough about things like fun and . . . well, love.

How does this relate to your financial plans? If you're thinking about how much you'll need to retire, don't get hung up on how much you'll need to buy the house of your dreams. But make sure there's enough in the budget to visit your children, pay your golf club dues, and maybe see a marriage counselor when things get bumpy.

Fear, Greed, and the Alternative

Back in 2009, about six months into the financial crisis that rocked world markets, author and radio host Krista Tippett hosted a series of conversations on public radio. She asked various religious thinkers, scientists, economists, and artists to talk about human values in the wake of the crisis.

Dr. Rachel Naomi Remen, a pioneer of the mind-body holistic health movement, talked about the crisis as an opportunity for spiritual inquiry. She saw it as a chance to ask questions like these: What can sustain me? What do I need in order to live?

Okay, let's ponder the first one: Will a bigger house sustain us? Or stronger relationships? Good health?

These are all, in a sense, financial goals. Obviously, a

bigger house costs more than a smaller house. Less obviously, staying healthy might mean spending some money on regular checkups, even if they aren't fully covered. Stronger relationships might mean spending a little less time at work—or even taking a pay cut—so that you can spend more time with your kids.

Remen and several other thinkers who took part in the series pointed out that our financial decisions often reflect our personal confusion or insecurities. If you think you're alone—if you're lonely—you may feel unsafe. If you feel unsafe you may look for ways to feel safer, to feel a part of your community. That might mean buying the same car and clothes as your neighbors, or taking the same expensive vacations they take. In the end, you won't feel less alone. Meanwhile, you may sacrifice your real financial security in your half-conscious attempts to achieve emotional security.

We talk about fear and greed as motivators, but you can argue that they're the same thing. Our greed grows out of our fear—and they both lead us to behavior that results in us spending money in ways that don't reflect who we truly are and what we really need.

The moral: whatever you have to do to gain self-knowledge, do it. Find out who you are and what you want. Then you can stop wasting your life energy and your money on stuff that doesn't matter to you—and start making financial decisions that will get you to your true goals.

Life Planning Versus Financial Planning

In the last few years, our public discourse—in the media, and in coffee shops—has begun to include discussions about money that get at deep questions. Who can you trust? Why do we need money? Ten years ago, most people would have considered this New Age Crazy Talk. Now it doesn't feel so crazy.

George Kinder takes a very broad approach to the notion of financial planning, which he prefers to call life planning. Life planning, he writes, aims to "discover a client's deepest and most profound goals . . ."

Kinder asks his clients three questions, which boil down to this:

First, imagine you are financially secure. How would you live your life? What would you change?

Next, imagine a doctor tells you that you have only five to ten years to live—but you won't feel sick. What will you do in the time remaining?

Finally, this time the doctor says you have twenty-four hours. What feelings arise? What did you miss?

As you work through the answers to those questions, you may learn something about what really matters to you. Most people's answers cite family and friends—relationships. Many responses cite authenticity or spirituality, creativity (people want to do things like write a novel or make music), giving back to their community, and connecting to places through nature.

Whatever answers you come up with, consider them when you make financial decisions. Chances are you'll make choices that better reflect your values.

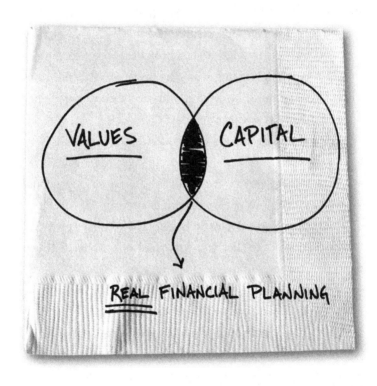

Self-exploration can be a painful process. Be patient with the process. Keep reminding yourself that it's not about the money.

It's about your life.

Urgent Versus Important

I'm writing these words at the beginning of spring. Even though there's still snow on the ground here in Park City, I suddenly realize that nearly a quarter of the year has come and gone.

Like many of you, I made resolutions in January. There were a lot of important things I wanted to accomplish. And for a few weeks, I did really well.

But now it's March. Part of me is panicked. There's still so much to be done. But another part of me latches on to the second half of the equation: I still have three-quarters of the year to go. What's the big deal?

Bob Goldman, a financial advisor, says that he sees a surge in business around January and February as people come in with their New Year's resolutions to update their investment portfolios or create their estate plans. So at least people are trying. But Mr. Goldman often doesn't see those people again for years.

Following through on the big decisions tends to drop down the list quickly when you're confronted by life's day-to-day demands. We all have a lot of things we want to do, need to do, and ought to do.

How can we handle these competing demands? It helps—a lot—when we distinguish between tasks that are

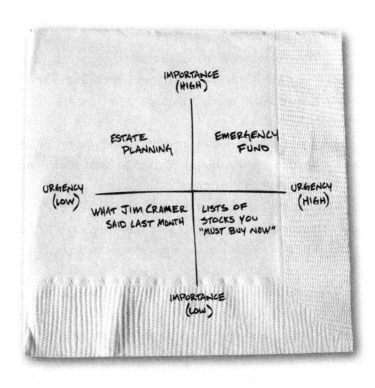

urgent (pressing, immediate) and tasks that are actually *important* (fundamental to our goals).

Some tasks are both urgent *and* important. They belong at the top of your list. Some tasks are urgent but not so important; still others are important but not so urgent. Typically, the ones that are urgent but not important get done. The phone gets answered. So does reading the Facebook posting from your high school classmate.

Meanwhile, the tasks that are important but not urgent drop to the bottom of the list and stay there. This can cause big problems. Dreams are awfully important, but they often don't seem urgent. And so our dreams fall to the bottom of our list.

You might need to fix the car—that's probably urgent, and might be pretty important. Shopping for a new surfboard? Probably feels urgent, but it's not as important as some of the non-urgent stuff that will affect your family's long-term security. (My surfer friends may disagree.) Clarifying who will take custody of your children if you die? Might not feel so urgent, but it can be awfully important.

On a day-to-day basis it's easier to focus on the urgent stuff, leaving the non-urgent but important stuff to wait. Which would you do first: get the car washed or update your will? The car is really dirty! The will? What's the rush?

What's more, updating your will—like buying life insurance or setting up college savings accounts—is a complicated process. Washing the car is easy.

We also enjoy the sense of checking urgent (not always important) things off a list. Some urgent tasks (shopping for that surfboard!) are even fun. By comparison, sitting down and working through the details of your personal and financial lives may not seem to offer the same sense of excitement and immediate gratification (though it can).

Of course, the important eventually becomes truly urgent. But by then it may be too late to do much about it. Think about the stories of friends and colleagues who are dealing with complicated estates because family members let the urgent trump the important. Then there are the parents who didn't think eighteen years would pass so quickly; now they're unsure whether they can help pay for college.

A friend who is an estate-planning attorney noted that people often come to him in a panic right before taking a trip without their kids. With worst-case scenarios on their minds, these couples want their wills done in case the plane goes down or the ship sinks. Since estate plans take time, it's often impossible to finish before they leave town. And then my friend doesn't hear back from the parents again ... until a few days before the next trip.

See a pattern here?

Schedule time each month to tackle these important but seemingly non-urgent questions. You will be tempted to brush them aside until next month. Don't.

After every financial crisis we often ask, How did we miss the signs? In fact, a large-scale financial crisis can be hard to predict, let alone prevent.

By contrast, a personal financial crisis is almost inevitable unless you address the truly important tasks in your life *before* they become urgent.

TOO MUCH INFORMATION

MARKETS are touchy. Last winter, a friend of mine was sitting in an outdoor bar on the beach in Central America—a place called Sol y Mar. My friend was talking to a guy named Gritty, a military veteran and an electrician.

The television over the bar was on, and some talking head was saying that oil prices were up because of chaos in Libya. Gritty told my friend (who has followed financial markets for thirty years) that that was stupid.

Libya? Hell, they don't supply much of our oil. There's something else going on . . .

My friend thought about it and decided Gritty was right. I agree.

Here's what Joshua Brown wrote for a blog called *Money Watch Africa*:

"Although Libya is a net exporter of crude [oil], it is only the seventeenth-largest source of oil globally, with no direct exports to the United States. Thus the concern from investors that Libya could cease to contribute to oil production seems overblown. . . . OPEC [Organization of the Petroleum Exporting Countries] and other oil-producing states could absorb the deficit by increasing their own production. . . ."

Okay. But maybe investors were worried that protests would spread to a big oil producer like Saudi Arabia. Or maybe people just freaked out, or they sold because they worried that *other* people would sell.

The point is: who knows? Not me. Not even Gritty (although he may have his theories).

Pondering this, I am reminded of how one piece of information can lead to a whole story based on greed or fear—which can get us into big financial trouble awfully quickly.

We sometimes deviate from our plan in response to a bit of news that may not mean what we think it means. Some of us have made it a habit to watch the news for clues about what we should do.

Wow. What a truly bad idea *that* is.

Remember: you only have control over certain things. Pay attention to what's happening, but don't overrate its significance to you and your plans.

With that in mind, are higher oil prices a signal to revamp your investment portfolio—even assuming they are going to stay high?

No.

The *Economist* Smirk

I don't know what it is about reading *The Economist* that makes some people feel like they are somehow smarter than the rest of the world—but it does. I was a subscriber for a while, and I always felt that just having the latest issue in my office, maybe lying on my desk, made me smarter.

Like I knew something everyone else was missing.

Recently I discovered that there is an *Economist* smirk. This smirk suggests that you have a secret, that you are part of an elite group who think deeply about the issues and have the information they need to navigate the world more skillfully than other people.

I shared this *Economist* Smirk Theory with a good friend

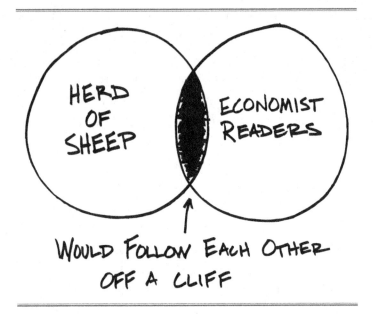

who happens to be a loyal *Economist* reader, and she thought it was silly. She doesn't smirk while reading *The Economist*; she smirks only when she sees someone reading *Time* or *Newsweek instead* of the *The Economist*.

Of course, the whole idea that something you read in a magazine (or see on television or hear on the radio or encounter on the Internet) is a secret is ... dumb. *The Economist* sells more than a million copies ·a week. A whole bunch of people think they are being clever in exactly the same way at exactly the same time.

And yet often we're tempted to act on some investment advice we come across in the media—as if we have come into possession of an important secret; as if we somehow have this idea that we were the only ones watching television that day. *Better act quickly before anyone else finds out about this!* Unfortunately, they already did find out.

Everybody's Doing It

Maybe we want to think we're uniquely in the know because on some level we understand that when it comes to investing, following the crowd can be costly. After all, when everyone is buying something, it's probably expensive (and therefore risky to own). And when everyone is selling something, it's probably cheap (and therefore potentially appealing).

We know this, and yet we feel safer in numbers. When we do what everyone else is doing, we can take comfort in knowing that even if we're wrong, we'll be wrong with a bunch of other people.

This kind of behavior—following the crowd—can have disastrous results. It led investors to load up on tech stocks in the late 1990s, bonds in 2002, and real estate in 2006. And yet we keep doing it, and the behavior gap grows.

That Magazine Is Not Your Financial Advisor

I love magazine covers about the markets and the economy.

One of *Newsweek*'s forays into the dangerous territory of predictive covers came in the spring of 2010, when the magazine boldly declared that "America's Back." The article pointed to a number of positive (but short-term) indications that the economy was recovering: job creation, productivity, and the Dow's 70 percent rise.

As it turned out, their pronouncement was faulty. The

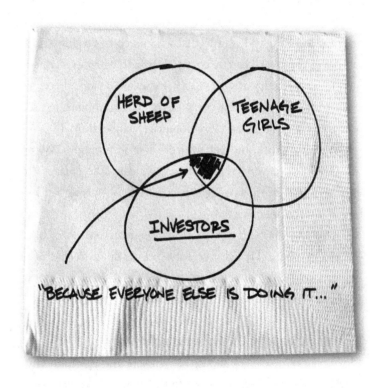

economy stumbled again, and continued to struggle as we headed into the fall of 2011. But the real point is this: you shouldn't make investment decisions based on what you see at the newsstand.

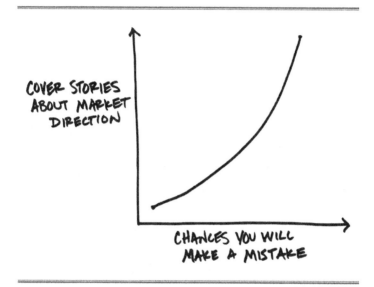

Let's think about this for a second. If you sold when things were bad (Remember? Back when almost all the magazine covers were declaring the end of the world?), you missed out on big market gains. When a magazine says "America's Back," is it time for you to move your money back into the (much higher) market?

If you ever find yourself out of stocks and considering getting back in because things look better, be careful. The fact that you sold when things were bad (many others did, too) is valuable information. No matter how good things look right now, the time will come when the market corrects again.

What are you going to do then?

Maybe the fact that you sold the last time things got rough is telling you something. Maybe you need a plan you can stick to—one with less investment risk.

On the other hand, if you didn't sell—if you make your investment decisions based on your financial goals—then what do you care what a magazine says on its cover?

I don't know what constitutes a bad or good time to invest. The point is that it's always a good time to stop the cycle of selling low and buying high. Who cares what *Newsweek* says? Focus on your goals. Build a plan that has the best shot of getting you there, and then turn your attention to living now.

You will be happier for it. (And richer.)

Ignore (Almost) Everything

People who learn that I run a wealth management business and write about personal finance immediately start asking me questions—usually about the stock market.

Maybe it goes like this:

New acquaintance: *So, anyway, what did the market do today?*

Me: *Um, sorry. I can't tell you.*

New acquaintance: Puzzled silence.

Me: *I mean, I'd tell you if I knew. But I don't know.*

New acquaintance: More puzzled silence.

Or like this:

New acquaintance: *Where do you think the market is going?*

Me: *Gee, I have no idea. Sorry. Not really my thing.*

New acquaintance: *Oh, sorry. I thought you said you ran a wealth management business and wrote about personal finance. . . . What do you do, again?*

It's bad enough that I don't know where the market is going. People are still more confused when they find out that *I don't even care.*

A frustrated family member once asked me about the market's prospects. I gave my usual answer.

His response: "So what exactly do you do if you don't follow the stock market?"

I told him that I help people make smart decisions about money so they can build and protect their wealth over time. I told him that this work doesn't require me to care about what the market did today or where the market will be in the future.

I added that, believe it or not, the ability to build and protect wealth is often inversely related to knowing what's going on in the market. And it's certainly inversely related to acting on that knowledge.

I told him what I tell my clients: it's a terrible idea to try to predict the market's movements. Monitoring market moves, watching stock market shows on CNBC, and poring over financial forecasts take a lot of time. Worse, it makes people anxious—and anxious people often screw up.

Think about it: ever try doing *anything* when you're anxious? Calm is always better.

What happens to anxious golfers? Jack Nicklaus says

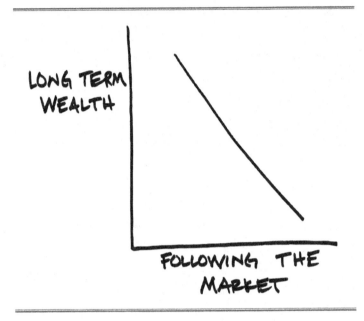

LONG TERM WEALTH

FOLLOWING THE MARKET

that very few people hold the club lightly enough. A friend who tried to teach me to play golf told me you should pretend you're trying to hold a baby bird. When you get anxious, you grip the club more tightly—and suddenly you're shanking shots all over the place.

What happens to anxious kayakers? The first time I got in a kayak—in the Snake River outside of Jackson Hole—I was struck by how important it was to keep my hips loose. When my hips were loose, I could move with the boat. As soon as I got anxious, I got stiff—and as soon as I got stiff, the boat got tippy.

What happens to anxious investors? When you start focusing too hard on market moves, every little ripple can flip the boat. Anxious people tend to buy high (they're worried because they're missing the big gains) and sell low (they worry the losses will keep piling up).

Anxious people seek comfort in familiarity. For example, they load up on shares of their employers' stock—which may in fact be quite risky. Or they buy a stock just because they've heard of it or know its products.

Anxious people get stuck in the past. Let's say you lost money in a stock. You know you'll feel better if you can just get back to even—but the stock keeps falling. Now what? More anxiety. More bad decisions.

Monitoring the stock market's ups and downs makes us anxious.

Trying to predict the future makes us anxious.

Anxiety can make us poor.

Too Much Information!

I admit that gathering the information we need to make rational decisions can help reduce our anxiety. But too much information can make our anxiety worse.

There's been a lot of chatter recently about the impact of technology on our lives—in particular, the way that it makes it possible for us to be connected to data all the time. We can check the performance of our stock portfolio in the middle of the night, on vacation, at our daughter's wedding . . . and we do!

Why is that? What's so compelling about all this data? How does it help us? Hurt us? I think these are important questions.

THE BEHAVIOR GAP

Not long ago, the popular blog *BoingBoing* ran an interview with independent game designer Jonathan Blow. When asked about one popular game (it's called FarmVille), Blow explained that the game wasn't designed to make players feel good.

It's supposed to look cute and project "positivity." But the game designers' real aim is to get people to worry about it when they're away from the computer. That way, they'll be drawn out of their real lives, and go back to the game.

How often does thinking about money make you feel this way? Watching CNBC daily or checking in with Bloomberg on a regular basis rarely helps you feel better in the long term about your financial decisions. But you keep worrying, and checking, and worrying, and checking . . .

My phone contains feeds from all my favorite news sources, hundreds of podcasts, all my email newsletters, and a bunch of books. Now whenever there is a spare moment of quiet, I almost automatically fill the space with data. I'm like a sugar addict in a candy store. It's just too easy to grab some.

It is becoming harder and harder to separate the signal from the noise. Most of us want to know what's going on in the world. We feel like it's our duty to be informed citizens, to watch the world markets, to stay on top of politics, and to keep up with the wide world of sports. If we don't, we might miss something or be left out of the conversation.

Unfortunately, the sheer quantity of information makes it virtually impossible to sift through all the noise (most of it is just that) and find the stuff that actually matters. Worse, we're losing our ability to distinguish between the two. What matters? What's just noise?

Free Your Mind

Researchers in recent years have found that what we think about can actually change the structure of our brain, so that patterns of thought become habitual. The more we worry about the market, the more we worry about the market—and the more we think it matters.

This means that checking the performance of our investments or the financial markets can become a sort of compulsion. The more we indulge in it, the stronger it gets. At a certain point, we become addicted to information that we hope will make us feel better. Trouble is, it often makes us feel worse—and eventually, we act on our fears.

Money isn't the only thing at stake here. I remember a *Wall Street Journal* article that talked about the impact of technology on our family relationships. One quote jumped out at me: "Technology should be on the list of the top reasons why people divorce, along with money, sex, and parenting."

The solution: change our habits. We need to spend less time watching and worrying about our money—less time giving in to our anxiety, our need to control things. If we can do that, we'll soon realize that it's not important to know what happened on Wall Street this week. What matters is what we did or didn't do in order to move closer to our goals.

Meanwhile, if we free our minds from clutter, we'll get back in touch with our real goals and what we can do to meet them. We'll have more time to connect with family and work that matters. We'll feel a greater sense of personal fulfillment. When I consume less information, my sense of well-being increases. The less I know the better I feel.

Try it. The next time you turn on the news, think long and hard about how you want to act instead of just reacting. In fact, think about whether you really need to watch the news that day.

You'll find that it's pretty easy to catch up when you miss a day or two. When the Dow hit 12,000 in early 2011 (before it dropped again), there was a great deal of media discussion about what this benchmark meant for investors. But who really cares? It's just a number. We all might as well have skipped it.

I'm saying turn it all off and go *do* something.

Here's an idea: try going on a media fast. Make it a point to avoid reading, watching, listening to, or thinking about information related to the economy or the financial markets or your investments. When thoughts about the market arise, let them go. Go for a bike ride.

Maybe go on a vacation where you can't get email or phone service. But don't be surprised if you go through withdrawal. There might even be physical symptoms. I once spent two weeks on an island off the coast of South Carolina during a stressful time in the stock markets. After a day or two without access to news, I came down with a really strange rash. There were two doctors on the trip. They claimed that it might have something to do with media detoxification. I'm still not sure if they were kidding or not.

Even a full day makes a difference, but take a few days off if you can. After three days with no cell service, the need to reach for my phone starts to ebb. There is a sense of spaciousness and time, and I can feel my anxiety abate.

Tuning out could even become a habit.

I know this may seem like a scary idea. And for the record, I don't support sticking your head in the sand. I just think you need to balance your money anxieties with perspective. Check the news or listen to the daily market report if you must, but don't make it the focus of your day.

If you must think about money, think about your goals—the things that really matter to you. Something crazy is always happening on the other side of the world, but what does that have to do with you? You can't do anything about it. You—and the world—are better off if you focus on what you can do.

Let's say you want to send the kids to college. Great idea. Tracking the performance of the Dow this week is not going to help you reach that goal. You'd be better off checking in with your kids to see how they're doing in school.

This same idea can apply to any of your financial goals. Yes, you will feel anxiety at times. Life happens, and you wonder if you've done enough. Stocks fall, and maybe you kick up your savings rate.

But don't let your fears run the show.

I repeat: almost none of that stuff on CNBC matters. Nothing bad will happen if you miss the endless commentary on the latest Fed announcement, I promise.

If investment success is truly about behaving correctly

over the long term and choosing investments within the context of your plan, what happens in the market day to day should have no impact on your decision-making.

Try it. See what happens when you turn off the noise and pay more attention to what's happening right now, right in front of you.

Awareness Beats Anxiety

Gathering information—being in the know—is not the same thing as being mindful, being aware, being present for what's actually going on behind the news and the chatter and the stuff that just doesn't matter.

Often when we think about money, it's in terms of either past mistakes or worries about the future. Both of those types of thoughts take us away from focusing on the present.

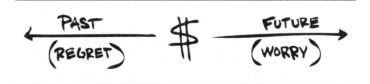

Many people have a tendency to beat themselves up when they make a financial mistake. But most of us should spend less time worrying about things we could or should have done differently.

Instead, we can use our experiences to help ourselves and others avoid similar mistakes without getting involved in feelings of blame or feelings of shame. We can look at our mistakes, make note of the lesson, and move on.

Spending too much time worrying about the future can also undermine our enjoyment of the present. This is a tricky issue for me because my work often involves encouraging people to have more meaningful conversations about the role that money plays in their lives—and normally such talks revolve around plans for the future.

One solution is to draw a line separating the time that you spend focused on planning for the future and the time you spend living for today. Planning for the future is very important, but it needs to be done in isolation to avoid overshadowing the joy of today.

Think about setting aside time each month to evaluate your recent financial behavior. Try to identify any mistakes you may have made, and note the lessons that you need to learn. Think about your goals and what you should do now to move closer to reaching them.

Once you've done that, get on with living your life.

Money decisions are emotional decisions—and making good money decisions requires emotional clarity. So try to pay attention to your emotions around money. This can be as simple as considering how you feel when you get your monthly investment statement or when a medical bill arrives in the mail. Acknowledging those feelings and being aware of their potential impact on your decisions can be important, often in ways that aren't clear right away.

I've found myself asking some really fundamental questions during the last several years. Who I can trust? What's really important to me? What do I really value? How much is enough? How should I really be spending my time?

I've watched as close friends have lost their businesses, their homes, and even friendships over money. I've seen friends struggle to find jobs at a time when they had planned on being well into retirement. Other friends have had to move parents into care facilities that fall short of their family's hopes but are all that they can afford. I've seen my own children's disappointment when I had to tell them that we couldn't afford something they really wanted.

When we go through these experiences we can feel sorry for ourselves and get angry.

Or we can try to understand past mistakes, practice self-awareness, and act from our deepest instincts.

Which approach will bring us closer to reaching our most important goals?

PLANS ARE WORTHLESS

THE notion that plans are worthless probably sounds funny coming from a guy who makes his living as a financial planner.

But it feels really good to say it in public, so I repeat: *plans are worthless.*

There are a number of reasons why we're hesitant to spend time planning for our financial future. It's time-consuming; it makes us anxious; we're not sure how to do it.

But I think the most important reason is a subtler one. I think we have confused the process of financial planning with its supposed end product: a financial plan.

Financial plans are worthless, but the *process* of financial *planning* is vital. A plan assumes that you know what's going to happen—even though you don't. By contrast, *planning* in its truest sense is a reality-based process that allows for life's unpredictability. It requires us to make decisions based on what's actually happening, rather than making decisions based on what we hope or expect or fear *will* happen.

A traditional financial plan starts with a bunch of assumptions. These assumptions typically are about factors such as future rates of inflation, what the stock market will do, how much you'll save, when you'll retire, how much you'll spend in retirement, and even when you'll die.

If you've been through this process, you know that it feels uncomfortable. One reason for the discomfort is that we know that no matter how hard we try to make accurate assumptions about future events, we will be wrong.

We don't know that inflation will average 3 percent annually, or that the stock market will go up 8 percent annually, or that we'll be able to save 10 percent of our pay (or what that

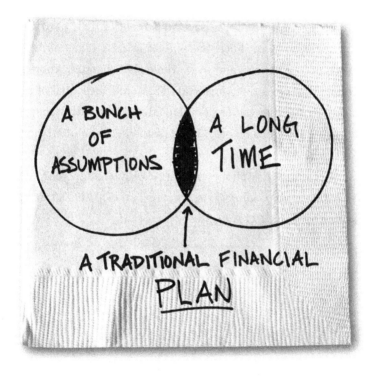

pay will be), or when we'll retire (we might not get to choose), or how much retirement will cost, or even when we'll die (at age sixty-one? seventy-eight? ninety-two? thirty-seven?).

Time after time I see clients whose lives have changed dramatically—for better or worse—totally derailing their plans. A couple decides to save 10 percent of their $180,000 income each year. Then the wife's business takes off, and their income doubles and their whole plan changes. Another couple organizes their financial life around their goal of retiring to Panama, but one of them falls in love with someone else and they get a divorce. Job losses, inheritance, bull markets, grandchildren . . .

Let's face it: a phone call can utterly change your life, your plans, your obligations, your resources. What's the old saying? *You plan, God laughs.*

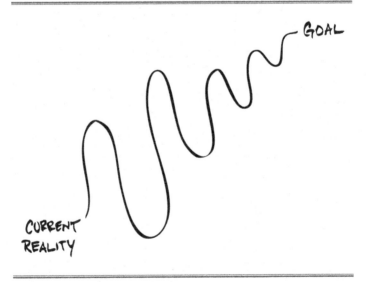

When I look back on my own experience, financial surprises are the rule—not the exception. My family and I moved to Las Vegas in 2004. We bought a house for $575,000. The guy who sold it to us had paid less than $400,000. The home's value rose to more than $1 million in 2007, at the height of the Las Vegas housing boom.

I didn't build a financial plan based on the assumption that Vegas real estate would continue to appreciate. Good thing. By the time we moved back to Utah (the move itself was also a surprise), the Vegas housing market had collapsed, and we owed the bank more than the house was worth. We had to work out a deal with the bank: we sold the house for $425,000, and they forgave the rest of the debt.

Wow. Talk about a surprise. We certainly didn't plan on the house going from $575,000 to $1 million. And we didn't plan on the value plummeting, either. There is no way we could have anticipated either event. Surprise!

Starting in the late nineties, a friend of mine built a business from scratch; he began it in his basement. He had potential buyers looking to pay more than $50 million for his firm. Based on that, he started working on plans to fund a charitable foundation to help educate children. Then the boom busted, and his business was worth $1.5 million. Not a tragedy—and he's moved on very successfully—but meanwhile he had to make some course corrections.

Another friend married a guy who had inherited a fortune. The husband managed to spend it on fast cars and high living. He unexpectedly inherited another $8 million or so from a distant relative. He spent some of that, too—

and lost most of the rest day-trading behind his wife's back.

Now she's in her sixties and looking for her first job. Not what she planned . . .

This is one of the cruel ironies of trying to create a plan of any sort: you don't have the information you need when you start. This means that your plan, whatever it is, will be based largely on more or less plausible fiction—or even outright fantasy.

Optimist, Pessimist, Realist

There's a syndrome I call Retirement Story Hour. A couple worried about retirement goes to a financial advisor. The advisor creates a plan based on various assumptions, and the couple finds that they'll fall short of their goals. They talk it over, and the planner moves some assumptions around. The couple finds that they are all set if they earn a bit more on their investments and retire a few years later. So they go back to behaving as they've always behaved—and secretly, they're still worried because they know the assumptions are basically nonsense. (Which brings me to another conclusion: *it's just fakery unless it affects your behavior.*)

Over-optimism is only one side of the problem. Sometimes assumptions can be too *pessimistic.* When you gaze into the future, you might find that at your current savings rate you'll never meet your goals—so you give up saving. But there's a very good chance that you'll be able to save much more over time. A writer I know was eking out a living in New York City thirty years ago, scrimping to save 15 percent of his (actually fairly modest) income in hopes that he could retire someday. He got sick of his job and left the city to move to the sticks and start his own publishing company—and it turned out he was good at it. Three years later his income had tripled; he has been semiretired since his mid-forties.

Pessimistic assumptions often discourage people from doing anything to improve their outlook. Your future holds positive surprises as well as risks. We focus so much on protecting ourselves from negative surprises (job loss, disability, divorce, death . . . the whole catastrophe) that we forget to factor in the positive ones (a raise, a business that works out, a new career, a bull market) that can sometimes change our entire outlook.

So remember: *good things happen, too.*

The point of all this is that all our assumptions are guesses. How much will we need in retirement? The answer depends upon inflation, tax rates, our health . . . the list is endless. And we can't really predict any one of those variables.

Years ago—more than a decade—I had a conversation with a friend who was a client. He and his wife had recently had a child. I asked him how much he thought he should save for her college costs. Here's what he said to me: "Hey, Carl, I have an idea. How about if I save as much as I reasonably can?"

My point isn't that we don't need to plan. We do need to plan. But if we accept the fact that even the best plan will turn out to be a fictional narrative about the future, we can focus our energy on the *process* of planning instead of obsessing over the assumptions.

The process of planning may—in fact, probably will—require us to chart a course that's headed in the direction we hope to go. That may involve making some assumptions about the future. But reality-based planning acknowledges that such assumptions are mere guesses. We make the best guesses we can. Then we can move on to the more productive business of investigating our current motives and circumstances, so that we can act from a place of understanding—not hope, not fear, but clarity.

I tell my clients that I'm giving them permission to let go of the need for precision in planning. Make the best guess you can and then move on. Put a stake in the ground thirty years out; think of it as a marker that you can always move later when you have more facts.

Think of the difference between a flight plan and an actual flight. Flight plans are really just the pilot's best guess about things like the weather. No matter how much time the pilot spent planning, things don't always go according to the plan.

In fact, they *rarely* go just the way the pilot planned. There are just too many variables. So while the plan is important, the key to arriving safely is the pilot's ability to make the small and consistent course corrections. It is about the course corrections, not the plan.

Two or three years ago, I climbed a mountain with a friend of mine. As we hiked up to the base of the climb, it started to rain. Other parties of climbers started to turn around, on the assumption that the climb would be wet and dangerous.

Brad and I had planned to climb a relatively difficult route, but now we decided to hike to the base of a different route—it's easier, and the serious climbing starts higher up on the peak. That meant we would be able to give the weather a bit more time to make up its mind (you know mountain weather . . . it changes).

As we climbed higher, more clouds rolled in. But it still wasn't dangerous, so we kept going. Eventually, we stopped behind a rock and brewed some tea and waited. The weather improved a little bit and we moved higher on easy ground. All this time, we were passing people who had turned around and headed down—but we kept going.

Eventually, the sun came out and dried off the rock. We roped up and headed for the summit. The climbing was fantastic, and we reached the top safely.

The experience was all the more satisfying because we knew that we could have easily turned around at the first sign of bad weather. Instead, we kept checking the situation and adapting to it. We didn't make up stories about what the weather was going to do. We watched the weather and worked around it. We ended up doing a different route—but we got to the top of the mountain.

Short-Term Planning for Long-Term Results

Once you have a general idea of your destination, the focus should shift to what you can do over the short term. Focus on the next three years. Thinking in shorter time frames inspires us to act based on what's actually happening. This is far more skillful behavior than worrying about what might happen in fifteen years (or even five). Remember: we just don't know.

That's why it's important to try to live in the present. The present is the only place we *can* live. When we live in the present, we are alert to what's actually happening—to us, and in the world at large. We can then act based on that awareness. And financial planning based on reality tends to lead to better results.

By contrast, when we live in the future, we're lost in fantasy or fear. When we live in the past, we're lost in regret or nostalgia. Financial planning based on fantasy, fear, regret, and nostalgia is likely to lead to more of the same.

Set a course, realize that you'll certainly be wrong, and plan on making course corrections often. Remember: the ongoing process of planning—not the plan—will keep you headed toward your goals and out of the behavior gap.

Investment Risk *Increases* Over Time

We often rely on past results to make our assumptions about the future. Seems reasonable. But even if the past can teach us about the future (and sometimes it can help), we face another problem. We have a tendency to misinterpret the messages that the past sends us.

Take our reading of risk. When people make financial plans, they generally spend some time and energy trying to decide how much risk they want to accept. At some point, if you spent any time hanging out with traditional financial services salespeople or in the investment section of a bookstore, you'll no doubt hear the claim that risk declines over time.

This story is often accompanied by an "educational" piece that looks something like the sketch above. The foundation of this story rests on the idea that over time, the range of potential investment returns narrows toward a long-term average of about 10 percent.

In other words, when you look at the best and worst returns for the stock market for any one-year period, you could
have lost over 40 percent or gained over 60 percent. That's a
really wide range.

But when you look at twenty-year periods, the worst average annual performance was a gain of around 3 percent,
with the best being about 15 percent. That's a much more
narrow range. Over thirty years, things get even closer to
the average.

The problem is real people in the real world don't really care about percentages. We care about dollars. No matter how hard you try, you can't pay for food, college, or retirement with a bucketful of percentages.

And guess what: when we measure the same range of potential investment outcomes in actual dollars, we get the opposite picture. The potential outcomes get *wider* over time.

How does it happen?

If you happen to earn 5 percent instead of the 7 percent you planned on, it will make very little difference twelve months from now. But in twenty or thirty years, you will end up in a greatly different place.

Again, flying provides a useful metaphor. Imagine a cross-country flight leaving from Los Angeles and heading to Miami. If you're a half inch off course when you take off, you will hardly notice when you fly over Las Vegas. Fail to make a course correction, however, and you run the risk of ending up in Maine instead of Miami.

If you base your plan on earning the long-term average return of the stock market *and* never make course corrections, you're at great risk of ending up someplace other than where you planned. On the other hand, if you set a course and then make slight course corrections when you find you have veered off, you can home in on your destination.

Financial Matters You Can Control

We're constantly bombarded by information: from reports of market ups and downs to headlines about nuclear accidents and overseas revolutions. But here's the thing: *no one really knows what these events really mean.*

When we come upon things that we don't understand, it can generate anxiety and fear. In our pursuit of control, we often obsess over the consequences of future events, even if they are almost always beyond our control.

So here are three things to remember when you feel like you have no control or understanding of how the world is about to change:

First, these things are not problems now.

When I start to worry about future events, I've found that it's helpful to focus on what's going on right now in my life. Often, I find that I don't have any problems right now, at this very moment.

To be clear, I'm not pretending it means that I don't have things going on that could have a significant impact on my life. Without question, we all need to deal with these types of concerns, but it helps to isolate that exercise from the reality of everyday living.

Second, focus on your personal economy and stop worrying about the global one.

There's much that's still in your control if you focus on your personal economy. That's why I love this quote from the investor Jim Rogers: "Any economy which saves and invests and works hard always wins out in the future over countries which consume, borrow, and spend."

When things get really complex, I find that it often helps to focus on my personal situation. I can still figure out a way to spend less than I make and invest in my skills or my business (over which I have a little bit of control). And I absolutely can get out there and work hard.

Forget about what's going on in China or global demand for the dollar or the price of gold. While we're worrying about those things, we could be doing things that actually make a difference in our financial lives—like working or trying to figure out how to save or earn a little more.

A similar principle holds when we get caught up in the idea that higher investment returns are the key to meeting our financial goals. Sometimes we even indulge in the notion that our investments will set us free from lives that don't satisfy us. We can quit our job, stop worrying, retire to Mexico . . . change the things we don't like about our lives.

But stocks aren't the lottery with better odds. Kicking up your returns probably won't dramatically alter your financial prospects, let alone your life.

Fortunately, you can do that yourself. While making wise decisions about how you invest your money is important, it doesn't have nearly the impact of working hard and saving more—let alone starting a business, going back to school, or reinventing yourself in any number of ways.

I'm reminded of a man I know who, back in his twenties, suffered from depression. He did a brave thing: he borrowed money against his house to pay for intensive talk therapy. Five years later, he felt good enough about himself to quit his dead-end job and start a career as an author. He's since sold a half million books and countless articles. He says therapy was the best financial investment he ever made.

I've found that it helps to think of earning money as my

job, and think of investing as a tool to *protect* the money I've earned. Of course that means that I might have to watch from the sidelines as the markets scream to new highs. But if taking this approach allows me to focus on earning more, starting a side business, or even just worrying a bit less, it may lead to a better result in the long term.

It's also important to remember that you have zero control over what the market does and at least some control over what you do.

The next time life starts to feel too complex and out of control, remember that you can get recentered by focusing on the simple (note: I didn't say easy) things you can do to impact your personal economy.

Wisdom Is a Financial Strategy

Here's an old Zen story. Two young fish swim past a coral reef. An older fish watches them from a distance, and he shouts across to them: *Hey, how's the water over there?*

The two young fish exchange puzzled looks, and one of them answers the old fish: *What the heck is water?*

The story makes me think of our relationship to money. We're swimming in a sea of money-related questions, worries, and hopes. But we're not fully conscious of the fundamental role that money plays in our lives.

The change in our relationship to money starts as soon as we realize how important money is in our lives. When that happens, we start to understand how important it is to make financial decisions that will free us from anxiety and confusion.

As our clarity grows, we can begin to put money into perspective. We may see that money is not a scorecard, let alone a guarantee of happiness. The amount of money we have says little or nothing about how successful we are as human beings, and it doesn't necessarily determine the quality of our life. It's just one of many variables, along with more fundamental ones such as skill, talent, generosity, clarity, love, luck . . . the list is very long.

In fact, our financial self-interest requires us to spend less time thinking and worrying about money so that we can focus on nurturing fundamental qualities—wisdom, health, experience, and so on—that can ultimately help us accumulate more money in the long run. (It's harder to make money when you're foolish, sick, and confused.)

Our deepest instincts (if we listen to them) will tell us that money doesn't *mean* anything: it's simply a tool to reach goals. And by goals I don't mean earning a high rate of return, outperforming the S&P 500, or finding the next great mutual fund manager.

By goals, I mean stuff that matters to you. Things like putting your kids through college, starting a business, becoming a yoga teacher, taking a year off, retiring at sixty, spending more time at home with your kids, buying a sweet car, kayaking the Grand Canyon, or helping your elderly parents.

Shifting your focus from a bunch of more or less incoherent worries about money to your genuine financial goals will clear your mind. You'll stop worrying about pseudo goals (picking the right investment) and lose interest in fake goals (owning a house bigger than your neighbor's, even though you don't really care).

That will free your mind to spend more of your time and energy (both mental and emotional) focused on what you really want—what actually matters to you. You'll start acting in ways that are consistent with your values, and act less out of confusion or fear.

Of course, you still have to think about ways to reach your goals. But that will be easier when you realize that your financial strategy is simply a means to an end (which you might call something like happiness).

Find Your Focus

You have only so much time and energy. You need to use it wisely. What to do?

My rule is simple: limit your attention to things that meet two criteria—they matter to you *and* you can influence them.

One of my clients is an older woman who lives in a rural community. She called me one day in a state of real anxiety about events in Lebanon. She wondered what those goings-on might mean to her portfolio.

I told her two things: *First—Lebanon isn't going to play a major role in what happens to you. Second—there is not a thing you can do to influence events in Lebanon.*

Then I asked her a question: *Given those two facts, why are we talking about Lebanon?*

I could tell you a hundred stories like that. I have two clients, married to each other, both physicians. They made it

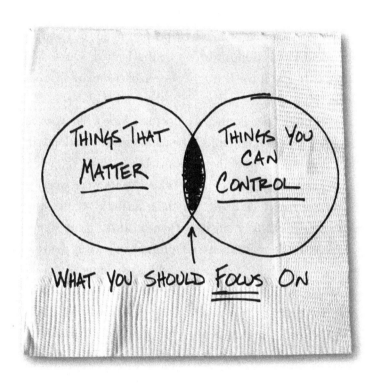

through the first year or two of this century just fine. Y2K, the dot-com collapse—those scares didn't bother them at all. Then came the 2003 SARS epidemic.

Remember SARS? The letters stand for Severe Acute Respiratory Syndrome. Back in the winter of 2002 to 2003 it killed more than eight hundred people, many of them in China and Hong Kong. No one in the United States died from the illness. It was a tragedy—one of the many that occur on this planet every day.

My young friends, the two doctors, were very worried about how SARS might affect their investment portfolio. In fact, they wanted out of the stock market.

It was strange. None of my other clients were worried about the impact of SARS on their financial plans. And SARS wasn't really a big deal from an investment standpoint. Even if there was some risk, there was no way to avoid it without derailing their plans—which would mean taking a much bigger financial risk. In short, even if SARS did present a financial risk, there was nothing they could do about it.

This is all very interesting to me. People worry a lot about things they simply cannot control.

The solution: focus on the things that matter to you *and* can be influenced by your behavior.

Forget the rest.

FEELINGS

FEELINGS can be expensive.

For example, holding on to investments for emotional reasons can cost us dearly. One of my clients, an eighty-two-year-old woman, was left with her entire net worth in a handful of individual stocks when her husband died. The stocks weren't suitable for the couple's portfolio when the husband was alive—and they certainly weren't suitable for an elderly widow.

I explained this to the widow, but she didn't hear me. Nothing I could say would get her to let go of those stocks. Her husband had bought them, and she had always trusted him. I told her that having 90 percent of your portfolio tied up in a handful of stocks is always a bad idea—and that it was an even worse idea for someone in her situation. She didn't hear me.

People's feelings sometimes convince them to hold on to their employers' stock even though it may be completely inappropriate for them.

You know how that goes. You're working for Company X, the company is growing, the stock is rising, you start to have visions of early retirement. You know you should sell some of the shares—after all, they make up 80 percent of your life's savings—but you hang on. This is fun! Besides, you believe in what the company is doing! You're reinventing your industry!

Then the company collapses and you lose everything—not only your job but your life savings.

That's an extreme example—but remember Tyco, Enron, and Lehman Brothers? How about GM? No one wants to believe the company they work for can fall apart, but

MISTAKES

EMOTIONAL ATTACHMENT TO AN INVESTMENT

sometimes it happens. I had friends who worked for Tyco—and they had no idea what was coming until it came. Enron? Jeff Skilling was a hero to many in the business community until shortly before the company collapsed.

When I tell stories like this to my clients, they nod sagely and agree that people who worked for those companies were a bit foolish to keep all their money tied up in their stocks. But then I try talking to them about their own company stock—and I meet resistance. (Just try talking an Apple employee into selling some of his Apple stock.) Time after time, I see people with most of their net worth tied up in their employers' stock. They're being loyal employees!

And so they put their retirement at grave risk.

Even more often, we hold on to investments just because we already own them. Inertia is a powerful force in portfolio management.

We are comfortable with the familiar. We've always owned a stock, so it feels right to continue owning it, even though we can't remember why we bought it in the first place. What's more, we know that if we sell the stock it might go up, and then we'll feel dumb. No one wants to risk feeling dumb—not when it's so very easy to do ... absolutely ... nothing.

Trouble is, doing nothing can be pretty dumb itself. You need to take a close look at your portfolio every once in a while, and make sure it matches your goals.

The Overnight Test

A friend of mine recommends what he calls the Overnight Test. Ask yourself what you would do if someone came in and sold all of your investments overnight. The next morning you wake up and you're left with 100 percent cash in your account.

Here's the test: you can repurchase the same investments at no cost. Would you build the same portfolio? If not, what changes would you make? Why aren't you making them now?

People have a tough time with this one. Maybe they've long since forgotten why they bought those investments in the first place (there must have been *some* reason, right?). It's kind of like certain relationships: you grow apart, your lives take different directions, and there's nothing much left to talk about . . . but you keep hanging around with each other because change would require work.

In the case of investments, you can't afford that kind of stagnation. You need investments that make sense given your current goals, which means you need to take a look at those goals, which means . . . work. This is why some people who take the Overnight Test just want to ask (Please!) for their old investments back. They may not admit it, but really they just don't want to do the work of coming up with new ones.

I understand. We're busy. We have a lot on our minds. Who wants to add another item (in this case, "review investment portfolio") to their to-do list? Unfortunately, this is one to-do that really needs to get done.

I'm not talking about change for the sake of change. Buying and selling investments costs money. I'm saying you need to know what you own, and why you own it.

Knowing When to Sell

How do you know when it's time to sell? I think about this question every time I hear people going on about big news on Wall Street—things like record-breaking earnings, company takeovers, or the latest IPOs.

Such talk was especially common in the late nineties. You remember the time. Everyone did well with their investments just by picking technology stocks or companies whose name ended with ".com." During that time, people often balked at selling their stocks because they didn't want to deal with the taxes on their (often enormous) capital gains.

They also believed—or wanted to believe—that their investment would keep rising indefinitely. If it could double, it could triple!

Emotions play a huge role in making the decision to sell—or not to sell. We don't want to pay taxes because it makes us feel bad to give up part of our profit to Uncle Sam. Or maybe we don't want to give up the fantasy that this particular stock is going to be the one that makes us, at long last, rich. Or maybe we just like being able to say that we own the latest cool (hot) stock.

But when we let our feelings get in the way of our direct perception of the facts (for example, the fact that a stock is much riskier now that its price has climbed), we get hurt. Sometimes we even suffer life-changing losses.

So if you find yourself with a few winning individual stocks, how do you make a decision that makes sense?

First, be honest with yourself. Let's say you invested in a stock at ten dollars, and it climbed to thirty dollars. Were you smart or just lucky? If you're being honest (which isn't always easy, since evolution has wired our brains for a certain amount of self-deception), you'll probably acknowledge that any triple-baggers in your portfolio reflect at least as much luck as skill.

Second, take the Overnight Test. Would you buy it now, based on the company's or the fund's prospects and price? (If you don't know, the answer is no.)

Third, review the investment's potential role in helping you reach your goals. Picking the next Apple is not a financial goal. Saving for retirement or having enough money to send your kids to college are financial goals. Once we're clear about the why—that is, about the goals that motivate us to invest in the first place—making investment decisions becomes much simpler.

With that in mind, ask yourself: Does this investment play a clear role in your portfolio? Does it add diversification benefits, a needed infusion of growth potential, or some other element to the mix? In other words, does it play a role in your efforts to reach your goals? If not, sell.

Fourth, walk away and don't look back. It's quite possible that if you make the decision to sell an investment because it doesn't align with your goals, the stock will promptly take off. Likewise, if you make the decision to continue to hold an investment because it does align with your plans, the investment may fall off a cliff, or at least trip on a curb.

With that in mind, you need to be emotionally prepared for the times when your faith in your perfectly sound, reality-based decisions will be tested. And of course, this applies to every investment decision—not just the decision to sell or not to sell.

Meanwhile, let's not make all this seem harder than it is. Making the decision to sell or hold an investment is relatively simple when we're aware of the cognitive traps of fear and greed. It should be clear to anyone that if you own an investment that has tripled in price, and you made that investment based on luck, it would be wise to take the profit and invest it in something that more accurately reflects your plan.

As usual, doing the right thing is simple. Maybe not easy. But simple.

Getting Stuck on a Number

One of the more common behavioral mistakes we make when it comes to investment decisions is the tendency to get stuck on a certain value or price. When we get stuck on a price, it can lead to costly blunders.

Let's say you paid $800,000 for your home a few years ago, and now you need to sell it. You want to get back at least as much as you paid. So you insist upon listing it for $800,000 even though you know the real estate market has come down. Three months later, you pass on an offer of around $750,000. Another six months later, you're hoping to get $700,000. That first offer looks like a dream.

Hey, guess what: the housing market doesn't care what you paid for your house. It doesn't care how much you put into it, or even what it cost you to landscape. All that matters is what it is worth today.

Here's another example: you buy a stock for fifty dollars a share, and six months later it trades at forty dollars. You know that it really doesn't belong in your portfolio anyway. But you don't want to sell it until you "get back to even."

This idea of holding on to an investment that is no longer appropriate, or may have been a mistake in the first place, makes no sense. The fact that you paid fifty dollars has no bearing whatsoever on what you should do now.

In fact, I think it is fair to say that getting back to even is *never* a good reason to hold on to an investment.

Yet one more example—the kind of thing I see all the time: your portfolio was worth $500,000 at the top of the market. You still think about that value each time you open your

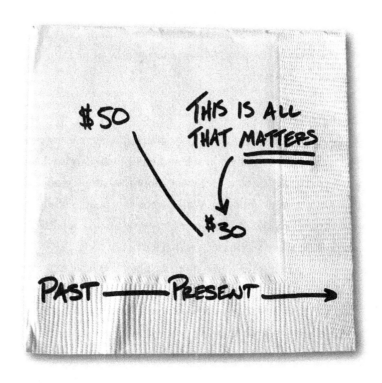

statement and see that your investments are worth less than that. You really, really want to get back to your high-water mark of $500,000. You occasionally find yourself daydreaming about it—like that guy next door still telling stories of his glory days playing high school football, when he should be out piling up victories or losses in some other pursuit.

The past is the past. What matters now is making the correct decision today.

The Dumb Money

We've all heard of the so-called smart money: the money that knows when to buy and sell and what to buy and sell. (It doesn't exist, by the way.) But what about the "dumb money"? That's what some folks on Wall Street call people who repeatedly sell stocks at a low price, only to turn around later and buy them for high prices. (That's most of us.)

Tired of being the dumb money? Then you have to make different choices.

The most important choice comes down to this: do we act based on what we know or how we feel?

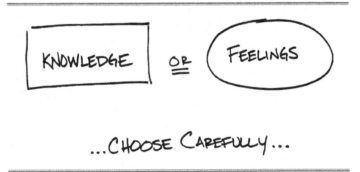

In an intellectual exercise, knowledge wins (buy low, sell high!). But in the real world, we're hardwired to pursue the things that give us pleasure or provide security, and run as fast as possible from the things that cause us pain. If that weren't the case, we would have been eaten by saber-toothed tigers a long time ago. This means that we're often driven by how we feel instead of what we know.

In December 2008, *The Economist* published a really striking cover, dominated by the image of a bottomless black hole in the ground. At the time I was struck by how well the image captured how I felt. When I saw it again in 2010, I had a surprisingly strong emotional response; the cover brought those feelings back.

The picture made me feel like everyone else did during that time: depressed and hopeless. I felt like a fool for not gathering what little gold I had left and hiding it under the house before it, too, fell into the hole pictured on the cover.

But here's the thing. While the picture captured exactly how I felt, I knew that acting on that feeling was a terrible idea. So I didn't sell.

Investment decisions should be made based on what we know, not how we feel.

So if you're thinking about making a sudden change to your portfolio, ask yourself if your decision is based on how you feel or what you know. Is it based on your feelings about what is going on in the market or is it based on an investment plan you put in place when you were thinking clearly?

There's an old saying: don't just do something, stand

there. When dealing with investments there is often this feeling that we should be *doing* something. A lack of action implies we're missing an opportunity or making a mistake. Cultivating a garden takes lots of hard work, but at some point you have to let the plants grow. If you have a plan, let it work.

If you're still convinced that you need to act, take a mandatory time-out. Write yourself a letter that explains what you intend to do and why. Pretend like you are trying to convince a wise friend that your proposed course of action makes sense. It might help to actually meet with someone you trust and talk it through.

Please. Ignore your gut feelings about the direction of the stock market. I can't tell you how many times I have heard people use their "gut" as an excuse to buy or sell stocks at what turns out to be just the wrong time.

I know, I know. It's not realistic to think we can remove all emotion from our decision-making. But we can work harder to make room for knowledge in our financial choices.

Uncertainty Is Okay

Investing, like life itself, forces us to make decisions in the midst of uncertainty. We will never be right all the time. We can control the process of making the decision, but we can't control the outcome. Investment decisions require us to make each decision based on available information: watch the outcome, consider new information as it becomes available, make course corrections—and repeat the process over and over.

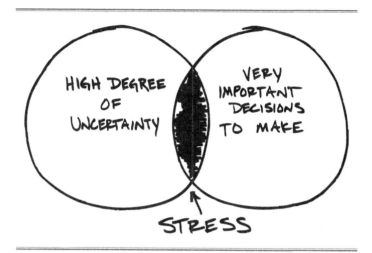

Most of the time, you shouldn't react to new information at all. But sometimes you should. How can you tell whether to act or not? Try asking these two questions:

One: if I act on this new information and it turns out to be right, what impact will it have on my life?

Two: if I act on this new information and it turns out to be wrong, what impact will that have on my life?

Just forcing yourself to consider the potential outcomes of being wrong will result in making much better investment decisions.

YOU'RE RESPONSIBLE FOR YOUR
BEHAVIOR (BUT YOU CAN'T
CONTROL THE RESULTS)

BERNIE Madoff spent most of the past two decades running the largest Ponzi scheme in history, defrauding thousands of investors of billions of dollars. Many of those investors were intelligent, sophisticated people. Some were top managers at major Wall Street firms. What happened?

Same old, same old. He promised the moon, and we wanted to believe he could deliver it.

There were warning signs. Many people on Wall Street had their suspicions of Madoff. A few were flat-out convinced that he was a fraud (and tried to tell the SEC and other regulators). Some Wall Street firms avoided doing business with the guy.

Others kept sending clients to him.

It would be nice to blame the whole thing on a few dirty rotten scoundrels. But that's too easy. Part of the problem lies with our almost universal tendency to believe what we

want to believe. It's really, really hard to resist a deal that looks too good to be true—especially when other people are buying into it.

I understand why people invested with Madoff. The guy had great credentials, and his record was very strong. Most folks didn't ask questions. They wanted those returns, and they trusted their advisors to protect them. Their advisors, in turn, trusted regulators. And regulators didn't get the job done.

Whatever. The fact remains that some pretty sophisticated people didn't nail down the facts before they put money (their own and/or their clients') at risk.

It happens all the time. Few people asked many questions when supposedly conservative bankers started offering high-yielding but risky new products to mainstream investors, like derivatives and securities backed by subprime loans. Meanwhile, we kept borrowing more money even as we sensed that no-money-down mortgages made very little financial sense. The banks offered us cheap access to money, so we didn't ask questions. We took it, and hoped for the best.

You, me, and most everyone else struggle to work up the nerve to question things that appear too good to be true. But as usual, it turns out that our financial security is our own responsibility. And sometimes, that means we have to be skeptics.

Chasing Income Is Bad for Your Assets

These days, I hear a lot from older folks who live off fixed incomes. They're worried because rates on bank CDs and money market accounts have declined, in some cases to virtually zero. They need income from their investments, so they're looking for higher yields wherever they can find them.

HIGHER YIELD = HIGHER RISK

A retiree will come to me, and the conversation may go something like this:

Retiree: *Hey, Carl, somebody told me about this really interesting new product. It yields 4.5 percent, and it's just like a bank CD. Shouldn't we buy a bunch?*

Me: *That's pretty interesting, given that twelve-month CDs are yielding around 1 percent. I wonder how this product can yield four times as much. Maybe we should ask some questions. Like, what are they doing with your money to generate those yields? Does this high yield come with any kind of guarantee from the FDIC?*

Retiree: *I don't know. They said it's like a CD . . .*

Me: *Hmmm. They did, did they? But here's what bothers me: if it's so much like a CD, how come its yield is so different?*

Retiree: *How should I know? I just need some income.*

The retiree could really use that 4.5 percent yield. After all, he has bills to pay. But that is precisely why he needs to be careful.

The more vulnerable we are, the more tempted we are to grab a great deal, no questions asked. But that can get us into big trouble fast.

Consider the market for bonds of companies with low-credit ratings—the so-called junk bond market. Junk bonds tend to offer high yields, because they're more risky than Treasury bonds. Every so often, the junk bond market reminds us that chasing yield is dangerous. And yet junk-rated companies sold a record $287.6 billion in bonds in 2010, even as potential borrowers with solid credit struggled to get home loans.

Investors were gobbling up junk because it offered higher yields than more creditworthy bonds. They weren't asking how those yields came to be quite so high. In fact, they didn't want to know.

If you push them, many investors will admit that they're unclear about the level of risk they're assuming in the investments they buy. But at some point, we have to learn to ask questions—hard ones—when we are presented with a financial opportunity, *especially* one that looks incredibly tempting.

It might help to remember one immutable law of investing: if the potential returns are high, the risk is also high. (Ask any economist.) So when returns are sky-high, so are risks.

The Myth of Unbiased Advice
It would be nice to think that your financial advisor's interests are always entirely aligned with your interests. But that's just not true.

Outright crooks like Bernie Madoff are the exception. Most financial advisors are trying to make a living by helping their clients.

Sometimes, however, those two goals are in conflict. That's okay—but only if we understand that the conflict exists.

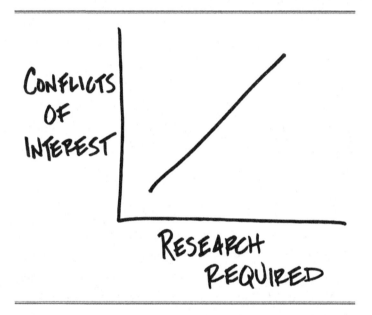

CONFLICTS OF INTEREST

RESEARCH REQUIRED

People often ask me to create a checklist that will help people choose a financial advisor. The kind of checklist they have in mind usually starts off by asking how the advisor is compensated. The idea is that if you know this, you'll know whether the advisor is likely to recommend unsuitable investments that will line his or her pocket (with commissions, for example).

Here's my take: conflicts of interest are inherent in almost any situation when you're paying for advice. Lawyers, accountants, financial advisors, auto mechanics . . . we all have to cope with situations when our interests may not fully align with the interests of our clients, at least in the short run.

Your job is to identify those conflicts, and then keep them in mind as you make your decisions. Think of it this way: when you walk into a Toyota dealership, you don't expect the guys there to tell you that Hondas are the greatest car around. You hope they're honest, but you know they're going to try to sell you a Toyota—and you make your decisions accordingly.

When you're working with a financial advisor, it does help to know how he or she is compensated. There are three basic models: You can pay by the hour for advice. You can pay a fee based on some percentage of your assets. Or you can hire a person who earns commissions selling you products.

Many advisors mix two or three of those models. Others limit themselves to a fee-only model; others rely heavily on commissions.

There is a great deal of debate about which model is best. The answer depends upon your situation—what kind of advice you need, your budget, and so on. And while the commissions-based model offers the most potential for conflicts of interest, no model can eliminate them. A fee-based planner may lose money when a client withdraws savings to pay down his mortgage, but it might be the right thing for the client. That's a potential conflict of interest right there.

What really sets good advisors apart is honesty. Are they open about conflicts, and do they manage those conflicts with integrity?

True, judging an advisor's integrity is not always easy. It takes time to develop trust—and in the early stages, you may have to work hard and spend a lot of time making sure you really understand the advice you're getting.

Over time you can streamline the process, but it should always be a partnership. Along the way, keep these points in mind:

First, Wall Street is in the business of selling stuff. That is its purpose on earth. It has a duty to shareholders to maximize profit, not necessarily share it with its customers. There are exceptions, but it's unwise to pretend that the people on the other side of the desk have a duty to put your interests in front of those of the firm that employs them.

Second, financial advisors are required to disclose to you the information you need to make educated decisions. Your job is to read and ask questions until you know what you're talking about and feel ready to make decisions. "Whatever you say" is not a good answer to the question "What do you think we should do with your portfolio?" A better answer: "I don't know; tell me what you think, and then I'll ask you about sixty-five questions."

Third, much of the advertising from the industry makes you think you are getting independent advice—but for the most part, you are not.

Financial advice comes from people whose interests are often in direct conflict with ours. And that's fine, as long as we recognize it. There is nothing illegal about trying to sell someone something.

Fourth, no one is forcing you to buy anything. Keep asking questions until you know what you're doing. Then, and only then, take action.

Hope Is Not a Budgeting Strategy

Maybe you've already learned this truth the hard way, but here it is again: the universe is not going to pay for that BMW you want.

That may surprise you if you're a fan of *The Secret*, which was a best-selling book a few years back. The book's premise is that you can create your own reality through your thoughts. If you focus intently enough on something, it will happen.

Many of us recognize that thinking good thoughts will generally make us happier and more attractive to other people. We also see some logic in the fake-it-until-you-make-it strategy. After all, how many of us are really qualified for the jobs we apply for?

But we can't change our reality simply by willing it— and the idea that we can is particularly dangerous when applied to money.

Using positive thinking to motivate ourselves to make healthy financial decisions is one thing. It's something else entirely to lease a BMW you can't afford and hope that the universe will make your payments because you thought about it really hard.

Maybe this sounds silly to you, but I see something sim-

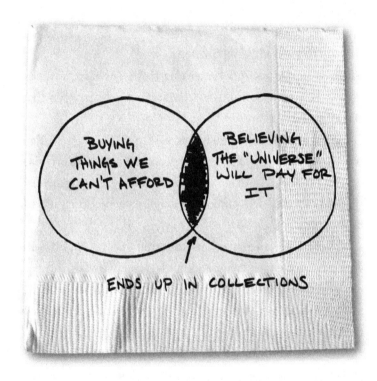

ilar happen on a regular basis. I routinely come across people who believe that getting to the next level, however they define it, requires faking it at an unsustainable level using material goods as part of the ruse.

For example, think about the people you know who believe that more expensive clothes or a flashier car will help them appear more successful, which in turn will help them close more deals or land that next promotion or project. The real question is whether there's anything to back up the flash.

Positive change requires hard work, patience, and discipline.

That's the secret left out of *The Secret.*

Investing Is Not Entertainment

We get into trouble when we confuse investing with entertainment.

A decade or so ago, investing had become America's favorite spectator sport. Everywhere you went people were talking about finding the next hot stock, mutual fund, or alternative investment. Magazines with covers like "Ten Hot Funds to Buy Now" and "Five Stocks That Sizzle" made investing sound fun. You couldn't turn on the television without seeing some lout screaming "Buy! Buy! Buy!"

Most of the stock market coverage in the media was designed to appeal to our fantasies about getting rich quickly—our wildest financial hopes and dreams. And most of us were eager to swallow the story that we could get rich quickly in stocks. So, despite knowing at some level that market timing,

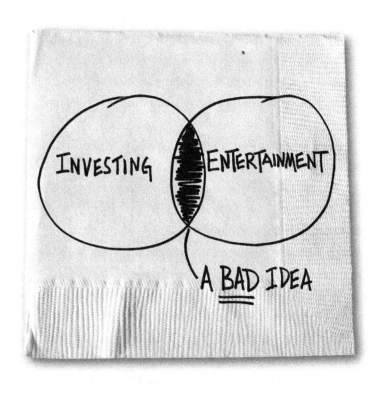

stock picking, and day-trading are hazardous to our wealth, many people still did those things.

Every one of those investors would have benefited from asking these questions: Am I investing to meet my most important financial goals, or am I investing as a form of entertainment? Am I being realistic, or am I letting my fantasies run away with me?

Sure, investing is fun while you're making money. And it's fun to indulge in occasional daydreams about getting rich the easy way. But this is not Monopoly. This is real life. We're dealing with real money and real goals. When we forget that—when we confuse investing and entertainment—we almost always end up behaving badly.

So next time you are tempted to "play the stock market" maybe you should go to the movies instead.

Whining Is Not a Financial Strategy

I'm pretty sure that the more time we spend complaining about the big banks and Wall Street, the worse our personal financial situation gets.

I realize that some people and institutions with financial power do things that are flat-out criminal, and they deserve to be punished. But what good does it do you to spend time brooding about their guilt? Wouldn't we all be better off devoting that energy to improving our own finances?

Complaining doesn't help. Sure, it might make us feel better for a while, or give us something to talk about at parties. But it can also distract us from the task of pondering our own contributions to the situation that is causing us pain.

Yes, it hurts to admit that we are partly to blame for our own losses. But it's essential to step up and accept that responsibility. When you acknowledge the role you've played in your own suffering, you can learn from your mistakes. If you simply blame others, you'll keep doing whatever you did and you'll end up in trouble again.

Whining sometimes reflects a mistaken belief that someone or something will (or should) always step up to save us from the consequences of our actions. This belief can lead us to engage in risky behavior. Why not? After all, someone will rescue us if we get in over our heads.

When friends, family, or government do bail us out of a jam, we tend to take even greater risks. (It's the "moral hazard" problem that economists talk about—in an era of bailouts, financial institutions take on more risk than they otherwise would.) Then, when things go wrong again and this time no one comes to the rescue, we feel betrayed. We blame others. We whine.

Don't get me wrong. I know there are situations where it really is someone else's fault. I realize that in many cases of financial hardship, family, friends, and the government need to step in to help. I have been on the receiving end of that kind of assistance myself.

As a rule, however, nothing will change until we make the conscious decision that we are usually responsible for our own financial situation. And even in those cases where someone else was clearly at fault, our energy is far better spent applying whatever lessons we can and moving on.

Lynnette Khalfani-Cox writes books about personal finance these days, but ten years ago she owed more than $100,000 on her credit cards. Bill collectors and repo men were a big part of her life. Her debt didn't reflect a medical emergency or a job loss. She'd simply spent freely, on everything from land investments to private school tuitions. In her words, she was earning six figures but spending like she was earning seven figures.

When the credit card companies stopped lending to her, she hit bottom—and then she decided to change her behavior. She cut her spending way, way down. She used every spare bit of cash to pay down debt. She doubled and tripled her minimum payments on cards. In three years she'd paid off $70,000; she sold some land to pay off the rest.

"The credit cards aren't the problem," she told one interviewer. "We're the problem."

Things started to change for Khalfani-Cox when she stopped complaining about the big bad credit card companies, learned the tough lessons, and took responsibility for her actions.

Feels Virtuous, Changes Nothing

To reach our goals, we have to look carefully at the things we're doing that we *think* are helping. In our pursuit of financial success we often get caught up in tasks that actually accomplish very little. Why? Maybe because they give us an excuse to ignore the bigger issues that will have a greater impact.

One cloudy day last winter I found myself driving out of my way to get some cheap gas at Costco. I didn't need a pallet of toilet paper or fifty gallons of milk, just gas.

THE BEHAVIOR GAP

While I was driving I started thinking about people's tendency to focus on certain areas of savings while ignoring others. The old idea of being penny-wise and pound-foolish really applies. If I saved ten cents a gallon on a twenty-gallon tank of gas, I'm up two dollars. That hardly covers the extra gas it took me to get there, let alone the time it took and the hassle of dealing with traffic.

DRIVING ALL OVER TOWN TO SAVE ON GAS?

AMOUNT YOU SPEND DRIVING TO COSTCO JUST FOR GAS

AMOUNT YOU SAVE BY FILLING UP AT COSTCO

False savings are a pretty common problem for some of us. See if you recognize any of these examples:

Doing your own taxes to save a few bucks. You might well miss out on potentially greater tax savings—as well as an organized and manageable accounting of your finances for the year.

Paying up for a car that will save on gas. Lexus makes a hybrid that gets an extra four to five miles a gallon but costs something like $30,000 more than the conventional model. My friend Barry Ritholtz, author of *Bailout Nation*, recently flagged a *Barron's* review of the hybrid. *Barron's* pointed out that if gas cost four dollars a gallon, it would take something like two hundred years of driving 15,000 miles annually to cover the extra cost of this hybrid.

Making investment decisions based on tax implications. A friend of mine worked for Oracle during the tech run-up in late 1999 and early 2000. The two of us were having lunch one day, and he told me he wanted to buy two snowmobiles. He didn't have the cash because all his money was tied up in Oracle stock—which had climbed sharply. He would not sell any of the stock because he didn't want to pay the 20 percent capital gains tax. The subsequent drop in the stock's value (it fell something like 50 percent) took care of that problem for him.

Institutions make similar mistakes. The IRS once sent two agents out to collect four cents of back taxes. Maybe they were trying to make a point, but still . . .

Sure, it makes sense to get gas at Costco if I am already there for the pallet of toilet paper. In some cases it makes sense to do your own taxes, and you might have your own reasons for buying the Lexus Hybrid. My point is that we need to focus on the things that really matter when we're making financial decisions.

You're Responsible, but You're Not in Control

While you're thinking, make sure you consider the bigger picture—the context of your behavior. A single action may have broader financial consequences that aren't immediately obvious. For example, you decide to start your own business. Your daughter works there in the summer and ends up running it. This could be good or bad—but it probably wasn't part of the plan.

You send your kid to Harvard because you think it's a good investment in her financial future—and she (bless her heart!) ends up teaching high school kids in an urban setting for $19,000 a year. This probably is not the outcome you expected. (Maybe it's the *right* outcome, but that's a different matter.)

Get it? You're not totally in control *even when you are making wise decisions.* So beware of making decisions for purely financial reasons. Instead, make decisions that square with your notions of virtue, wisdom, and common sense.

And remember: you're responsible for your own behavior—but you can't control the results.

WHEN WE TALK ABOUT MONEY

OUR conversations about money often leave us feeling confused, misunderstood, and even angry. Why is that?

One reason is that we use money as a stand-in for deeper issues we don't want to discuss. To take an obvious example, we may say we can't afford something because we are anxious about the future, or because we think we don't deserve the things we want.

It's easier to talk around these issues than to face and acknowledge our feelings. So we talk about (or argue about) the expensive leather jacket or the trip to the beach, when what we are feeling goes much deeper and is much, much more interesting.

Like religion and politics (which are also hard to talk about), money brings up uncomfortable feelings. We may feel guilty about spending money or get a huge thrill out of spending money—or both. We may use money to create a sense of safety and security: if I have enough money in my 401(k), I can breathe. We may use money to control people we love; or we may have a history of being controlled by people with money.

When someone says, "It's only money," they're usually wrong. Our feelings about money run deep, and they are often very complicated—and sometimes quite confusing. No wonder things can get pretty intense when the subject of money comes up. It breaks up marriages, families, friendships, communities—even countries.

Money conversations are also complicated by the fact that few people know much about personal finance or investing. Choosing a mortgage or even a credit card is a complex

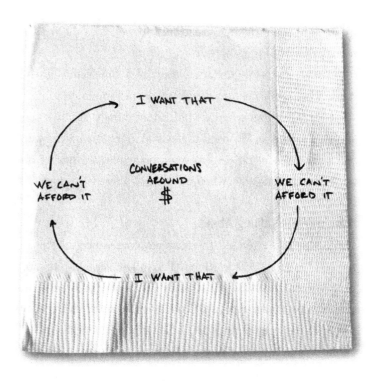

process these days—few of us are really qualified to decide between the products out there. The same goes for investments.

It's all pretty daunting, and we have a natural tendency to avoid things we don't understand. We are wired to either fly or fight in confusing situations. So we avoid the topic of money—or we fight about it.

Money is too important a topic to avoid—and fighting doesn't help. We need to develop a deeper understanding of what we talk about when we talk about money. And we need simpler language. We need to develop more straightforward ways of representing concepts and principles so that we can understand each other when we do have these conversations.

What's Worth Talking About

Awhile back, I attended the national conference for the Financial Planning Association (FPA) in Denver. Despite more than fifteen years in the financial industry, I'd never attended this conference, so I didn't know what to expect. I figured I'd encounter lots of people walking around with calculators discussing obscure financial concepts. Instead, I was surprised to find an amazing group of people engaged in meaningful conversations about the role of money in our lives and how to help people deal with complexity.

I walked away from the conference struck by how strongly meaningful conversations can affect our behavior. Although most of us have grown up with the idea that it's not polite to talk about money, everywhere I turn people are starting to do just that. They are asking questions that they've never asked before and rethinking assumptions they've long held as absolute truth. These questions are about broad issues, like trust, happiness, and the definition of "enough," and specific issues, like the definition of risk and fundamental assumptions about the stock market.

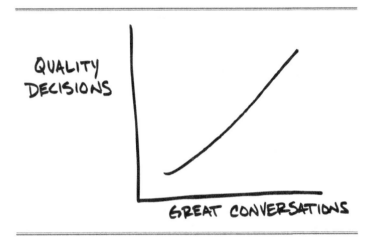

These are questions we should've been asking all along. There is a growing recognition that great conversations about money are really great conversations about life. This recognition includes acknowledging that the traditional approach of the financial services industries can lead to poor decision-making. Saving, budgeting, investing, tax planning, insurance, and estate planning should be related to the larger context of your life, your goals, and your values.

I believe one of the most important things I can do when faced with a financial decision is to talk to someone I trust: a friend, a family member, or a paid professional.

Start talking to people you trust about questions that matter to you.

What role does money play in your life?

What needs to happen in the next few years for you to feel like you are making good progress?

What money mistakes have you made in the past that you want to avoid in the future?

Too many of our financial conversations are about finding the best investment or best life insurance.

Try to talk about what matters to you.

She Says, He Says

If we are going to make good financial decisions, we have to make them in the broader context of our lives. That means taking into account our personal histories, our fears, our desires, our gifts, and our limitations.

The next time you find yourself in a discussion about money that feels emotionally charged and familiar, take a step back and ask yourself if it's really about money. What are you feeling? Can you talk about that?

I recently received an email from a friend highlighting this very issue. He admitted that he avoids money conversations with his wife because he doesn't feel like he has a good financial plan, which makes talking about money stressful.

For my friend and his wife, the absence of a financial plan has become the proverbial elephant in the living room. They know it's there—but they don't talk about it.

This happens to a lot of people. They're worried about

money, but they don't know what to do about it. So what's the point of talking?

Well, if you don't talk about it, nothing will happen. No, that's not quite right: things will get worse.

Of course, when you do raise the topic of money, things can get messy—at least for a while. For one thing, people have different takes on money matters. Our upbringing, our experience, our education, and our personalities can all play a role in how we talk and think about money. We all bring baggage to these conversations.

Unlike my friend, I don't avoid money conversations. I tend to start them when I shouldn't.

One day, my wife mentioned that her friend had recently redone her kitchen. As she explained all of the renovations, I started doing mental arithmetic that quickly added up to big dollars. Instead of engaging in a fun conversation about why my wife liked the kitchen and what she thought was cool about it, I responded with my typical "We can't afford that."

My wife gave me a confused look and said, "What are you talking about?"

Fifteen years of marriage, and I still haven't learned that when my wife talks about a new kitchen it doesn't necessarily mean she wants to remodel *her* kitchen. She was only discussing something of interest to her that she thought might be of interest to me.

This conversation isn't the first time that I've made the mistake of assuming my wife is talking about money when she's just talking about life. Every time she mentions someone she knows who is planning a family trip to Hawaii, I

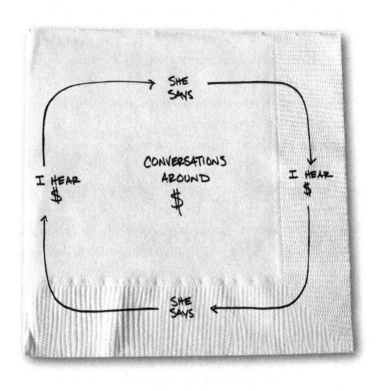

immediately start calculating how much such a trip would cost. Likewise, a conversation about where friends plan to send their children to college gets me thinking about money.

What I took as code for "I want a new kitchen" was just my wife talking about something she enjoyed. How many times has something like this happened between you and your partner?

I will probably continue to do mental arithmetic when I'm chatting with my wife, but if I remember that 99 percent of the time she's simply talking about subjects that interest her, I can reduce my anxiety over money.

This is not a question of who's right and who's wrong. Rather, it's an opportunity for us to recognize that we can't impose our views of money and our expectations about money on other people.

The elephant in the living room may look pink to you and green to your spouse. But you still need to talk about that elephant.

You and Me, We're Different

My premise that people can think and talk about money differently from each other upsets some folks—but the differences do exist. I'm not saying that all men talk about money one way exclusively and all women another. There's no way it's that simple.

But I will say this: money conversations between partners are often complicated by the differences between them—some of which may be gender related. (Are such differences universal? Are they caused by nurture or by nature?

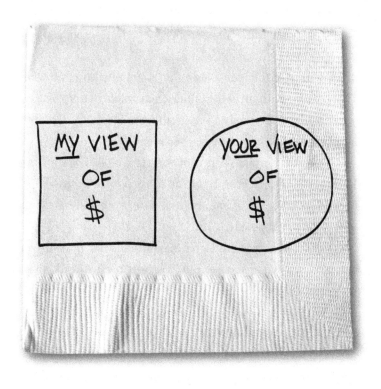

I don't know. But they do seem to exist in some circumstances.)

It's dangerous to pretend that we're all the same. Confusion about our differences can cause frustration and anxiety, and can even break up relationships.

A woman I know got married last spring. Her husband had a job, and she managed to get a new job soon after their wedding. They also got a good deal on a home.

A month into the marriage, the husband was laid off. His wife didn't worry much at first. He seemed confident he'd get another job, and once in a while he did get some short-term work. But nothing lasted more than a week or two. Worse, he didn't seem to be trying very hard to find something more permanent.

The wife was concerned. She began looking for a second job to boost their income. The guy's response: "Why are you so worried? I'll get something soon."

Six months later, the wife is in danger of losing *her* job and her husband hasn't found anything yet. In her words, he's waiting for the perfect job. He assures her that he's on top of the situation.

The couple also differs on the subject of debt. While she was raised to avoid debt as much as possible—buy older cars, don't rely on credit cards—he was raised in a relatively free-spending family.

Every time the wife expresses concern about their financial situation, the husband shrugs it off.

Who is right? Actually, the wife has a pretty strong case—the couple's financial situation demands attention—

but that's not the point I want to make here. I'm more interested in the fact that two people who love each other have very different takes on the same situation. The wife is very pragmatic—even a little uptight—about financial matters. Her husband is more relaxed—perhaps a bit reckless—about the same issues. And so they're talking past each other, and making no progress at all.

We all bring our personal biases to the table when it comes to money. We need to listen hard—maybe as hard as we've ever listened to anyone—to figure out where our partners are coming from.

At the same time, we may need to be aware of our own biases, and find language to express what we need and what we feel about money.

Of course, that kind of work can also help us to prepare for productive conversations about other issues as well. I'm saying that compassion and honesty are powerful tools in relationships. Practicing them can be a great investment in our shared financial futures.

I'm Okay. Are You Okay?

People tend to think that if you just follow a checklist of financial tips, you'll feel more secure. The reality is that what makes us feel safe depends on family background, education, work experience, and our general feelings about risk.

One conversation about financial security that I have witnessed many times demonstrates this. It's the debate over investing extra money versus paying down the mortgage.

One spouse says, "We should buy that stock." The other

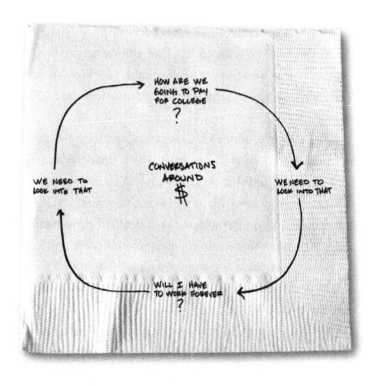

spouse says, "I want to pay down the mortgage." These conversations (which often turn into arguments) tend to take on more urgency during times of financial stress—and they can cause strains in a relationship.

Fortunately, you can avoid the worst strains and learn something about each other—but that requires you to listen. When you hear, "I want to pay down the mortgage," or "I want to buy more stock," take a minute to follow up with, "Help me understand why it's important to you that we do that."

These conversations are never easy, and they get harder for couples who don't know much about financial matters. It's even more difficult for folks who were raised to avoid talking about money. If that group includes you, you'll find it especially uncomfortable to have detailed conversations about the things that make you feel financially secure.

Sometimes you can come up with a solution by looking at the numbers—how much you need to save, when you plan to retire, and so on.

But, as you may know from personal experience, what makes us feel safe may be at odds with the numbers. Once again, as couples, we need to talk openly about what worries us and what comforts us.

Generation Gaps

Most parent-child conversations about money go like this:

Parent: *"We can't afford that."*

Child: *"Pleeeeeze . . . ?"*

And so on.

I think fear keeps us from having deeper money conversations with our children. We worry that such discussions will upset them or confuse them. Or we don't know what to say. We also may avoid these conversations out of habit, cultural norms, or family tradition.

There's no question that these discussions need to be handled with care, but we do need to have them.

A friend's recent experience with his oldest son captures my point. My friend and his wife always believed it was important for them to teach their kids that there are limits to what their family could buy. Like many of us, my friends made their case by falling back on the statement "We can't afford that" each time their kids asked for something.

After a few months of this, my friend's fourteen-year-old son asked him a question: "Dad, on a scale of one to ten, with one being homeless and ten being Bill Gates, how much money do we have?"

As they discussed their situation, it was clear that his son was asking not because he wanted to buy more things, but because he was actually worried about whether the family was okay.

My friend assured the boy that he didn't have anything to worry about, but explained that they didn't have unlimited money. They should spend their money on things that really mattered, and avoid buying things that weren't really important to them.

Okay. Makes sense.

Kids often know more than we think they do. They sense anxiety even if they don't make the immediate connection to money—and we can scare them if we say things we don't really mean.

We can't afford that is not the same thing as *We'd rather use our money for something more important.* The second statement shifts the debate from *Are we poor, or what?* to *What matters most to our family?*

What a great question.

SIMPLE. NOT EASY.

THE BEHAVIOR GAP

WE may say we want simplicity, but we tend to choose complexity.

Why the contradiction? We get caught between two competing stories. In the first story, we tell ourselves we want to simplify, simplify, simplify. In the second story, we tell ourselves that the solution to an important problem has to be complex.

On some level, we all understand that simplicity is the ultimate form of sophistication. As a climber, I like to read about the exploits of other climbers. The most admired people in the sport include people like Ed Viesturs and Steve House, who understand the value as well as the beauty of simplicity. They climb the biggest, scariest mountains with just the things they can carry on their backs—a huge advance over old-style expeditions that lay siege to a peak with an army of porters and piles of equipment.

Simplicity is both beautiful and functional. And yet people are often disappointed when I propose a simple solution to their investment or financial planning problems. Such solutions can often be reduced to a simple calculation on the back of a napkin. But people worried about money tend to take comfort from a sixty-page doorstop packed with charts, graphs, bullet points, and calculations.

This tendency to seek comfort in complexity even shows up in emergency rooms. A physician friend of mine tells me that patients are often disappointed when he offers a prescription that is relatively simple: "Go home and get some rest," or "Stop smoking and eat a little less junk food." Some

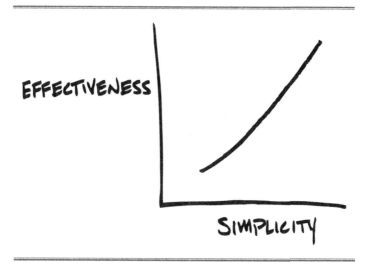

patients come looking for a diagnosis that will requires professional treatment (*Maybe I'll get surgery!*). They can't believe—in fact, they're disappointed to learn—that there is a
simple solution to their health problem.

Why the disappointment? You've probably guessed the
answer already: We often resist simple solutions because
they require us to change our behavior.

And so we spend $40 billion a year on weight-loss pro-
grams and products rather than take the simple, do-it-
yourself approach: consume fewer calories, burn more
calories with exercise, or do both. We'd rather look for a
magic bullet: something to save us from the day-to-day
grind of simply doing the work that needs doing.

I came across a Reuters article about a family who put
their kids through college with no debt. They managed it on
a modest income by driving the same car for ten years and

putting money away month after month. The author asks, "Is this a fairy tale?"

If we answer yes to that question, we've forgotten the basic tenets of financial success. Saving money, avoiding speculative investments, and repeating that process over and over may not be sexy, but it gets the job done.

Our attraction to complexity distorts the way we approach our financial goals. The simple options that have the largest impact on your financial success require discipline, patience, and hard work. They require that we apply those basic fundamentals over and over for years. It's much easier to entertain ourselves with the fantasy of finding an investment that will give us a fantastic return than to save a little bit more money each month. But in the end, the fantasy will fail us.

The work will deliver.

Gratification Can Be Painful

Some years ago, Amazon.com created a premium shipping program called Amazon Prime. For a flat rate, customers could get free two-day shipping.

BusinessWeek claimed that "Amazon Prime may be the most ingenious and effective customer loyalty program in all of ecommerce, if not retail in general." It converted casual shoppers, "who gorge on the gratification of having purchases reliably appear two days after they order, into Amazon addicts."

The words stayed with me: "gorge on the gratification."

More recently, I read an article in *Newsweek* about how Americans were spending again, whether they could afford

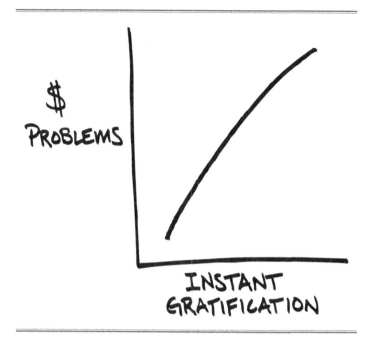

it or not. Just two years earlier, the media was claiming that an entire generation of people had changed their consumption habits and ideals based on the economic tumult they had experienced. But evidence suggests that many of us have already forgotten what it felt like to be pushed to the brink.

We all know the old saying that old habits die hard, and nowhere does this seem to be more true than with our spending habits. They are awfully difficult to change.

I'm struck by how often I encounter the phrase "American consumers" in my casual reading. At some point, it seems that we stopped simply being citizens and became consumers, too. Along the way, we bought into the idea that shopping makes us happy and that our spending is essential to shaping our identities as human beings. We're even told that—as a matter of patriotism—we need to spend more money to get the economy going.

Personally, I think the economy will be better served if we spend more carefully.

You and your family will be better served, too. In the sixties, researchers at Stanford University launched a decades-long study that looked at our ability to delay gratification. They found that people who've figured out how to postpone the fulfillment of their desires, instead of giving in immediately, experienced greater success than those who haven't.

You might object that budgets can be boring. But you have to admit that success is fun. So how can you keep more money in your wallet?

Try a mandatory holding pattern. Before you buy something, stop. Add it to a list and let it sit for three days. Then revisit the list.

It's amazing how something you absolutely had to have holds almost no interest after three days. I find this especially true with books. When I first signed up for Amazon Prime, I quickly found myself with a stack of books that I never started.

Now I use Amazon's wish list or shopping cart and let items sit. I have a very long list of books on my wish list that I have never ordered, and yet the world continues to spin.

Go on a multiweek buying fast. See how long you can go without spending any money beyond necessities.

This originally started for me when I entered every transaction into Quicken manually. I got sick of entering so many transactions, so I tried to reduce the number of purchases.

In a crazy way, this can be fun. See how few transactions you can have in a thirty-day period. If you use a credit or debit card, see how short you can make your monthly statement.

Track your spending. Do it. I know you're sick of hearing this suggestion, but you need to measure and track spending. (Use software like Quicken or Mint.) Things that get measured almost always improve.

Put a price tag on your goals. Do you have any idea how much it will cost you to send your child to college? How important is that to you? Is it more important than the plasma television today?

Take taxes into account. If federal, state, and local tax amount to 35 percent of your earnings, you need to earn around three hundred dollars to clear two hundred dollars. Find out your overall tax bracket and do the math every time you buy something. You might start to spend more carefully once you realize that you have to earn three hundred dollars to pay for that two-hundred-dollar dinner.

Think about what you'd earn if you invested the money instead of spending it. Let's say you spend six hundred dollars on a ski weekend. Now assume you had to earn nine hundred dollars before taxes to pay for that trip. What if you'd invested that nine hundred dollars in a 401(k) account? Don't give up skiing—heaven forbid—but maybe skip an occasional trip so you can more fully fund your retirement savings.

These are pretty simple ideas, but they require discipline. Simple. Not easy.

The Secret

A few years ago, I had an interesting conversation with a gentleman who had managed to turn a relatively small inheritance into a very large net worth. These days he spends his time fly-fishing on his ranch in Utah and surfing in Hawaii and that sort of thing.

He came to see me in my office on a snowy Utah day; he was wearing jeans and a down jacket, his typical winter garb. During the course of our conversation I asked him what his secret was. How had he managed to achieve such financial success?

He gave me a confused look. After a moment, he said, "Sorry. I'm not sure I understand the question."

I said that what he had done was very unusual, and I had thought there might be some secret that he could share.

His reply: "Carl, I just bought boring things and paid them off over thirty years."

The reality is that there is no secret. Just boring stuff like spending less than you earn, setting some money aside for a rainy day, paying down debt, and steering clear of large losses. That's it.

Simple. Boring. But certainly not easy.

Slow and Steady Capital

We have all heard the story of the tortoise and the hare. Slow and steady wins the race.

It's easy to forget this mantra when most of what we read in the financial press is written to sell magazines or drive traffic to websites. Slow and steady does not sell magazines or drive traffic to websites.

I've seen firsthand the damage investors inflict on themselves by chasing hot investments. And so I'm really interested in the idea of slow and steady investing. I love the term "slow capital," which I first heard from venture capitalist Fred Wilson. I would add the word "steady."

Slow and steady capital comes close to describing my ideal investment process.

Slow and steady capital is far more concerned with avoiding large losses than with chasing the next great investment. Being slow and steady means that you're willing to exchange the opportunity of making a killing for the assurance of never getting killed.

Slow and steady capital means you can have a life. If you accept the fact that slow and steady wins the race and you find a way to invest that way, you can turn off all the noise of Wall Street.

A client of mine worked in a hospital that backed up to some of the best trail running in the country. Doctors competed to work there because it was in such a beautiful place. My client never knew whether to laugh or cry when he would head out for a run in the mountains behind the hospital during lunch. On the way out the door, he'd see the other physicians—many of them trail runners themselves—huddled around CNBC, as if Jim Cramer was about to reveal the secret to endless wealth. Slow and steady capital allows you to ignore that noise and go running on those trails.

Slow and steady capital knows that the goal of investing is to accumulate the capital you need to fund your most important goals. If your goal is to have something to talk about at the next neighborhood party, try something else.

Slow and steady isn't easy. It always seems that someone else is getting rich quick. But take the time to look behind the stories, and you'll find something else.

I had a conversation recently with a prospective client who told me that he had done pretty well with an aggressive trading strategy. I have heard that enough times over the years to know that we all have selective and short-term memories. Sometimes it takes only a few winning trades for someone to forget the losers.

That was the case here. True, things had indeed gone well for my prospective client during recent months. But he had lost around 50 percent of his savings when the market slumped in 2008—so his growth was on a much smaller capital base. All things considered, he had a terrible investment record. Moral: if you decide to be slow and steady, remember to take with a huge grain of salt all those stories of people getting rich quick.

Slow and steady capital is short-term boring.

But it's long-term exciting.

CONCLUSION

THIS book isn't meant to be a step-by-step guide. I wish I could be more specific about how to solve your problems, but because I don't know you personally, I can't give you specific advice about your individual behavior gaps. Remember: taking financial advice from a stranger is dangerous.

But this book does provide a framework for you to start making better decisions about money. The first step is to take a deep breath and reflect on past decisions to identify where you can change your behavior. We've all made mistakes, but now it's time to give yourself permission to review those mistakes, identify your personal behavior gaps, and make a plan to avoid them in the future.

The goal isn't to make the "perfect" decision about money every time, but to do the best you can and move forward. To make those decisions, you also need to know where you want to go. Once you've settled on a destination, be it retirement, travel, or paying for college, keep making decisions that move you in that direction. You will need to make course corrections, but if you're clear about where you want to go, it becomes a lot easier to close your behavior gaps.

The goal isn't to make the "perfect" decision about money every time, but to do the best we can and move forward. Most of the time, that's enough.

ACKNOWLEDGMENTS

This book has been the result of a really wild, almost magical series of happy accidents. Keep in mind what we are talking about here: a financial planner in Park City, Utah, who uses a Sharpie and cardstock to communicate complex money issues. Who in their right mind would want a seat on that train? Lucky for me there was an army of people just crazy enough to encourage such behavior.

Marion Asnes was among the first to see the value in the work I was doing in a quiet little corner of the financial planning community.

Ron Lieber took a chance by including me as the first ever (and I am certain the last) Sharpie-wielding contributor to the New York Times Bucks blog. The belief Ron had in my ability to get at the emotional core of financial issues served as a light even when it was dark.

Christy Fletcher's belief in my work and ability is a real inspiration. I think of Christy not simply as my agent, but as a partner and friend.

I'm not sure there are many people like Clint Willis still around. A fantastic and accomplished writer, he was not only willing to help with the good old-fashioned editing but actually really enjoyed the process of making sure I told the story I was trying to tell.

One of the highlights of my professional life was the Friday afternoon that Courtney Young called out of the blue to ask me if I had considered writing a book. I still remember I was sitting in the parking lot of my local ski shop about to pick up my freshly waxed skis and head out for a lap or two on the Nordic track. It's one of the few phone calls that would cause me to put skiing on hold.

I had a quiet dream of working with Portfolio on a book someday, and the experience more than lived up to my expectations. Courtney and the entire team have been awesome. Thanks go to Eric Meyers for the patient reminders, Will Weisser for his keen insight, and Amanda Pritzker for getting the word out. It is a real pleasure to work with you all.

This section of the book was the only part where I missed a deadline, and it was because I could simply not figure out how to express my thanks to Britt Raybould. What do you say to someone who has worked on a project (especially when you are the project) for years, often not knowing for sure if it would ever pay off? Part project manager, editor, shrink, coach, and always a trusted friend. I guess you say THANKS!

The paradox of those I consider my really good friends is that they often left me with the impression that somehow I was helping them when it was not hard to see that I always end up on the receiving end in these relationships. This is certainly true with Brad Petersen, Jason Slatter, Matt Hall, Veruan Chipman, and John Stephens. Thanks, guys!

The conversations I have had with an amazing group of clients at my wealth management firm informed almost every page of this book. I'm super grateful for their patience and trust . . . something I do not take lightly!

One more thing . . . I have an amazing MOM (yes, that should be in all caps) who is always looking out for me. I remember the first time I wrote something for the *New York Times* and the comments section got pretty intense, it was my MOM who called and asked if I was going to survive all those "mean people." It's great to know that she is always there watching out for me. Thanks, MOM!

Printed in the United States
by Baker & Taylor Publisher Services